"At New Leaf we are blessed to have the opportunity to interact with numerous authors of books that help people achieve harmony, balance, health and spiritual fulfillment in their lives and relationships, and to have the opportunity to help these books reach the people who can benefit from them. Recently I had the privilege of receiving a new book by Michael Goddart called "A New Now" in which he surveys virtually the entire range of daily life and activity and provides key insights to help people navigate the issues they are facing in their lives.

There are countless areas where he has presented positive ways to make a difference in the way one feels, thinks, and interacts, and even taking up just a few of these ideas would be beneficial and highly worthwhile for people seeking for answers to the concerns and problems they are facing. Michael's prior book was well received and has won a number of awards. I expect the new book will get a lot of positive support from those who take some time to read and reflect on what Michael has to say.

As the President of New Leaf Distributing Company, I do not often have the opportunity to interact closely with specific books that we distribute, but I am very glad that I had this chance. Thank you, Michael, for your clear and concise writing and insights to the human condition, not just in generalities, but with specific help for people facing just about any situation."—SANTOSH KRINSKY, PRESIDENT, NEW LEAF DISTRIBUTING COMPANY, LITHIA SPRINGS GEORGIA, WWW.NEWLEAFDIST.COM

"*A New Now* delivers on its promise to guide the reader through the thought-maze of mind to mindfulness; unpleasant psychological states to equipoise; spiritual darkness to the experience of one's soul in the Now. Goddart's guiding voice throughout is both wisdom-filled and profoundly practical...and obviously road-tested by himself. If I were shipwrecked on a tropical island and were allowed to bring only two books, one would be *A New Now*. (The other? *Admiral Haggerty's Guide to Small Boat-Building*!)"—ELIOT JAY ROSEN, AUTHOR OF THE *Los Angeles Times* BESTSELLER *Experiencing the Soul—Before Birth, During Life, After Death*

"Michael Goddart's latest book, *A New Now: Your Guide to Mastering Wisdom Daily, Achieving Equilibrium and Empowering Your Nobler Self* is filled to the brim with very helpful advice about how one can better navigate the twists and turns that invariably arise in one's day-to-day life. What I found most remarkable was how one can feel the author's guiding presence throughout the text which is both warm and encouraging. It is not a book about judgments or regrets, but rather developing new stratagems based on sound biological, psychological, and spiritual principles in order to achieve one's desired wants and goals.

A New Now is a comprehensive guidebook that touches on all aspects of one's life with remarkable clarity. This is the type of book that you will want to keep by your bedside and read from daily. In a world that desperately needs to rediscover a natural harmony and unity, Michael Goddart's A New Now offers us a road map on how we can all become wiser and more compassionate. This book will resonate with anyone, even those without a spiritual bent, who wish to live a life of optimal flourishing. It is rare indeed to find a book that contains so much wise counsel."—DAVID CHRISTOPHER LANE, PH.D., PROFESSOR OF PHILOSOPHY, MT. SAN ANTONIO COLLEGE, FOUNDER OF THE MSAC PHILOSOPHY GROUP

Take the Most Fascinating Journey

In Search of Lost Lives

Winner of the Living Now Book Award
Winner of the Body Mind Spirit Book Award
Winner of the National Indie Excellence Award
Winner of the American Book Fest Best Book Award

"*In Search of Lost Lives* is a brilliant exploration of a soul's journey through many past lives. Imagine how different our lives and our world would be if more of us had access to this kind of knowledge. Michael Goddart has given us an invaluable gift."—RAYMOND A. MOODY, JR., M.D., PH.D., AUTHOR OF *Life After Life*

"As we humans ascend the spiral of evolution it becomes more evident that we cannot do so without multiple reincarnations. Methodical inquiry and research is slowly building the case for this aspect of conscious evolution but detailed personal accounts of successive lifetimes are practically nonexistent. Pythagoras is said to have recalled all of his former lives but unlike Michael Goddart he left no record for us to examine. *In Search of Lost Lives*, Goddart's sweeping narrative, allows us to contemplate a journey through thousands of lives in the quest for complete spiritual liberation—which makes this book a significant and timely contribution to an exciting and important field." — J A M E S O'DEA, FORMER PRESIDENT OF THE INSTITUTE OF NOETIC SCIENCES, AUTHOR, ACTIVIST AND MYSTIC

"Michael Goddart illuminates the transcendent experiences and spiritual purpose of so many lives that I got a true sense of his spiritual evolution from the beginning when he dwelt on the first of his three planets to his present life when he is on a dedicated spiritual path with a Teacher." —DR. RAJIV PARTI, M.D., AUTHOR OF *Dying to Wake Up*, CONSULTANT IN CONSCIOUSNESS-BASED HEALING

A NEW NOW

Also by Michael Goddart

In Search of Lost Lives: Desire, Sanskaras, and the Evolution of a Mind&Soul

Spiritual Revolution: A Seeker's Guide; 52 Powerful Principles for Your Mind & Soul

BLISS: 33 Simple Ways to Awaken Further

A
NEW
NOW

*Your Guide to Mastering Wisdom
Daily, Achieving Equilibrium, and
Empowering Your Nobler Self*

MICHAEL GODDART

Clear Path Press
Rhinebeck, New York

Paperback ISBN 978-1-951937-73-7
Hardcover ISBN 978-1-951937-74-4
eBook ISBN 978-1-951937-75-1

Library of Congress Control Number 2020921283

Book and cover design by Colin Rolfe
Cover photograph by Simon Matzinger

Clear Path Press
c/o Epigraph Books
22 East Market Street
Suite 304
Rhinebeck, NY 12572
(845) 876-4861
epigraphps.com

to those who seek a better now

"He taught that we are all greater than we know
and that wisdom is the path to salvation."

—Larry Darrell in *The Razor's Edge*
by W. Somerset Maugham

Contents

CHAPTER SIX

The Ten Keys to Achieving Equilibrium
The Second Five Keys

· 144 ·

CHAPTER SEVEN

The Five Sources of Wisdom

· 164 ·

CHAPTER EIGHT

The Eleven Evolutionary Wisdoms

· 192 ·

CHAPTER NINE

The Five Prerogatives of Equilibrium

· 223 ·

CHAPTER TEN

A New You

· 231 ·

CHAPTER ONE

A New Now

Why This Book?

You have been given the most precious gift—your human life. Before you know it, it will be over. Why not make best use of it?

You may be doing your best to get through each day, but messages you absorbed, knowingly and unknowingly, from family, friends, religion, therapies, and even social media may be impeding your way. You may be living with a tangled amalgam of conflicting impulses or ways of being that do not serve you or support who you are and who you can become. You were born to realize your fullest potential.

Philosophers and writers from Epictetus, Montaigne, Emerson, and beyond spoke and wrote about how to live. The ancient Greek injunction to "Know thyself" is crucial to living your best life, your fullest self.

By engaging with your awareness, you develop your inherent wisdom and powers of knowing, and ultimately step into a new reality. You have the capacity to live on a higher plane. You have an authentic self that can be freed and empowered.

By working with this book and engaging your consciousness

throughout the day, you will step into a new reality, a new now. The benefits awaiting you are many. Here are some:

- Centering and focusing of your energy
- Clarity of mind
- Choice and enrichment of relationships
- Enhanced creativity and productivity
- Enlightened direction of health and healing
- Being present
- Development of intuition
- Happiness each day
- Grooming of your destiny

As you free and empower your authentic self, your will and willpower will clarify and strengthen to meet challenges that greet you. Also, you will learn to muster the spiritual strength, discrimination, and qualities necessary to engage with each situation. You won't be at the mercy of negative emotions. Rather, you will be able to choose to let go of expressions of anger that might otherwise run you. The benevolent emotions you experience will inform your life, like a suffusion of warm sunshine breaking through an overcast sky. You will gain a keen awareness that will observe, negotiate, and choose to be at the cause of your unfolding life, rather than its beleaguered victim. Ultimately, this all will be expressed naturally and automatically, moment to moment.

Does this seem like an impossible dream? Do you doubt that you have the potential to bloom into your wisdom? That's okay. You can doubt and at the same time nurture the belief that you can achieve all this and more.

The essential question is: How can I live as my aware self? If you ask yourself this question and explore it, realms of possibility open. One pathway to the authentic you is to live with wisdom.

Working with this book will help you become wiser, achieve a state of equilibrium, develop a clearer and stronger sense of your purpose, and travel through your days as fully conscious as possible moment to moment, so that you begin to experience *a new now*, now and now and now. This is moving toward being truly alive.

Why Wisdom?

Webster's Third New International Dictionary first defines wisdom as "the effectual mediating principle or personification of God's will in the world." Wow. How can this be understood? The archaic definition of mediate is to form a connecting link. Synonyms are "conveying" and "conciliating." Effectual means characterized by adequate power to produce an intended effect or result. In this sense, Wisdom (capitalized) is the connection between our all-knowing Source (God) and us. By growing in Wisdom, we express more of the divine, the *intended* divine, God's will. That's inspiring.

Aspects of wisdom include insight, knowledge, sagacity, virtue, prudence, judgment, and sanity. Wisdom is utilizing the best of your mental and intuitive faculties moment to moment.

Wisdom can be defined simply as the comprehension of knowing. Knowing is something that is apprehended or you take possession of in your awareness. *Webster's* defines knowing as "the condition or fact of possessing understanding or information or of being aware of something."

Is it a coincidence that the word "know" is "now" preceded by a *k*? To know is to comprehend the now. Many sages have said or written something to the effect of: "Now is all we have." The letter *k* comes from the Greek letter *k* (kappa), which was taken from the Semitic *kaph*, the symbol for an open hand. To know is to open your hand to receive the now.

The species of human beings is *Homo sapiens.* This is from the Latin *homo*, "man," plus *sapiens*, the present participle of *sapere*, to be wise. As a member of the species, by being wise you are fulfilling your birthright and your ability to master reality.

Another way wisdom can be understood is the capability of apprehending reality in your awareness. The more wisdom you possess, the closer you are to omniscience. Being omniscient is having infinite awareness, understanding, and insight; knowing all things; spontaneously accessing perfect wisdom. This is your divine birthright.

If you embark on your journey of mastering wisdom daily, you will be able to move sleekly toward becoming the best you that you can be. You can know better *how to live.* That's how best to live, for *you.* As you learn to handle astutely whatever difficulties and challenges arise, you can begin to master the art of living. You can make decisions that best serve you and others. You can evolve, knowing automatically: what next? You will be able to avoid all kinds of unnecessary involvements that otherwise would fill you with fear, uncertainty, anxiety, and negativity. You will also be able to avoid captivating attractions and false shoulds that divert you from your true path.

The mastery of the art of living is in how well you negotiate the challenges that come and the impulses and demands of your mind. As you progress with this mastery, when you make free time and ask yourself the essential question— "How can I live as my aware self?"—you open the door to ideas and possibilities.

Developing your wisdom is a way of taking charge of your life while, at the same time, aligning yourself with your higher consciousness. In this way, you are attuned to those quicksilver nudges that come unbidden from that consciousness. And because you have been pulling the weeds of negativity, tilling the field, and sowing good seeds, you are more likely to notice these intuitive, supremely helpful intuitions and act on them.

Life is tough. At least, that's the way it feels much of the time to many of us. But you can also look at it as an ongoing journey in which, to navigate well, you need to use all of your wits. As we progress from babies to infants to children and then on to teenagers, young adults, and mature adults, we grow in our ability to navigate. Some progression in wisdom is naturally taking place. But we have vast, untapped resources of knowing what to do when. Each of us has a benevolent, higher, better self that we can learn to open to more and more.

Imagine that your consciousness is an inverted well of knowing. Think of it as an aquifer. An aquifer is an underground layer of water-bearing permeable rock. Think of strata rising in your field of awareness with the spaces between the strata as pure consciousness that can filter down to your everyday present awareness. Believe that you have an infinite, inexhaustible aquifer behind your eyebrows that you can access and which will flow through to you. The conscious work you do with your-self accesses that "liquid" higher consciousness and dissolves the rock that is holding it back.

Gaining better and better access to your inherent well of knowing transforms your life. It gives you assurance, free-dom from anxieties, sure purpose, readier achievements, and happiness.

You can master wisdom daily, at your own pace. You don't need to disrupt your life and attend expensive retreats. You can integrate your own private course into your daily life. In fact, this is the best way to master wisdom daily.

To practice and master wisdom daily, you will need to observe what is going on within you—your feelings, thoughts, flashes of intuition, changes in bodily sensations—and what is going on around you—especially interactions with people. You can learn to be a detached, discerning observer of your life rather than be pulled from one impulse to the next, unknowingly. It's not difficult—you're simply devoting a bit of awareness to observing. Exercising your observer awareness is a muscle of awareness you possess and may or may not have developed. Your observer awareness is your friend and an element of your consciousness that you can trust and let guide you to enhanced richness and satisfaction and a life truer to who you are *and* to who you are becoming.

Thus, the way to master wisdom is to *teach yourself.* Working with this book, read a section, be aware of it, and apply it to feel-ings, thoughts, situations, and actions as they arise. From time to time, when you are prompted—intuitively or mentally—read a particular section or return to it, and know or figure out how you can apply it to your life. If you are so moved, write notes that you date and can access later.

How many times have you read an inspiring and practical book only to forget its key revelations and lose the opportunity to integrate its wisdom into your life? If you only read a book, you may remember one to three things and, if you don't forget them, to what extent would you incorporate them in your life? That's why to profit handsomely from this experience and bring about real change, you might want to keep a journal. You could call it your "Journey Journal."

The Journey Journal is the means by which you can gain the most value from this book, by choosing what you want to work and play with and recording key lines from the book and your experiences, reflections, and goals. You can also enter what you intend to practice and enter the page number of the book that discusses it. Then after you do practice it, you can write about it. Although your creative juices may flow better if you write by hand, if the entries are typed (after your handwriting or initially) and searchable, you'll be able to find your observations, experiences, and states of mind and relate them to where you are presently.

You can create a section for items you would like to attend to in the future with references to your journal and/or the book. When you read a section that triggers a response such as curiosity, ideas, memories, or hopes you want to explore, you can also practice freewriting either by hand or typing. Freewriting is letting yourself go to write whatever you feel like, knowing that it can and will be free of others' scrutiny and your own judgment.

Freewriting is meant to be freeing, opening your expression to feelings, higher knowing, and inspiration.

If the name Journey Journal does not appeal to you, you might wish to call it Now Notes, Experience Journal, Wisdom Journal, or simply Journal or Diary. Choose whatever feels best and resonates the strongest for you. This is your personal, private journey. If you'd like to keep your journal entries organized in the applicable chapters and sections of this book, you can download a Word file of "Contents" in Free Media on my website (goddart.com).

If you keep a journal, it can be a valuable tool in facilitating growth. It's something you can return to and read to help make sense of your life journey and purpose. Every step you take toward mastering wisdom is positive and allows you to evolve into the being you are meant to become. Along with learning to master different expressions of wisdom, learning to achieve equilibrium will greatly facilitate your mastery of wisdom.

The Power and Potential of Equilibrium

Equilibrium is dynamic balance, a spiritual center that you can live in and learn to return to again and again. Being in a state of equilibrium is wonderful. It enriches your life and helps you feel good and supports your health.

What are the characteristics of equilibrium? Here are five key ones.

➢ Quiescent ego
➢ Even temperament

> ➤ Grateful contentment
> ➤ Healthy independence
> ➤ Balanced desires

Quiescence is a state of repose, being tranquil. When your ego is quiescent, it isn't raging for something it "needs" desperately. When your ego is quiescent, it isn't inflated, self-justifying, self-pitying, or wallowing in injury. It isn't driving you to take actions or say things that aren't in your best interest. Being unaware of your ego, letting it ride roughshod, is self-defeating, knocking you about in *dys*-ease. The antidote to ego is humility—welcome, revitalizing oxygen.

When your temperament is even, you are not anxious or angry, negatively critical, upset, leery, or fearful. Your instincts are accessible and you're open to inner promptings. You realize that most people are entirely run by their minds and have no control over what they say and do. People who are run by their lower minds do, say, and write things that are unkind, hurtful, stupid, destructive. Their actions can readily set off your reactions, which can be angry, fearful, or one of their myriad expressions, such as annoyance and worry.

Have you ever felt or thought that you have everything this moment that you need? One aspect of wise, clear thinking is not mistaking where you think or hope you're going for where you are now. With contentment comes acceptance. You may yearn to understand what you could do with the rest of your life, but embrace the perfection of who you are now and the intention to take each next step in your life as consciously as possible. Acceptance is a key element of consciously living in reality. Acceptance is not resignation. It's being here, now, rather than allowing yourself to be run by envy or disappointment. Grateful contentment is a feeling of ease, of peace, of everything in its own time. Regardless of your circumstances, if you attain periods of grateful contentment, more and more, in your state of equilibrium, you will cherish these simple, luxurious feelings.

When you are able to live in a state of healthy independence, your life is not ruled by attachments. You realize that everything is ultimately temporary. People must leave your life and at times that can be unexpected. You are not the center of the solar system, with everyone revolving around you. You have a great storehouse of resourcefulness that you can access to enable your life to proceed well without unhealthy neediness that inhibits your growth.

When your desires are not inflated or squelched down, you are aware of them, and moving at the right time and speed toward realizing them in a way that serves your growth and unfolding. We are desire machines—the mind is constantly spewing out desires. You can learn to be aware of how your desires want to drive you, and you can mentally detach from them, as well as you can, and make mental adjustments that balance your urges and put them in perspective. Being the driver of your desires creates more space for gratitude. By cultivating mental detachment from your desires, you can more readily be present in an expansive now in which you can experience a healthy independence and grateful contentment.

Wisdom and equilibrium go hand in hand. Being in equilibrium is an optimal state in which you can best access your power and develop your potential. You more readily enjoy a positive, confident attitude because when you are in equilibrium that comes naturally. You can more easily deal with and rise above distractions. Being in equilibrium and learning how to achieve and return to it is a necessary adjunct to mastering wisdom. It facilitates the accessing and growth of wisdom.

The more you realize and embody the five characteristics of equilibrium, the more you reduce stress. Tomes can be written on the benefits of reducing stress. Some doctors believe that stress is the root of all disease. Some spiritual masters say that ego is the root of all disease. Stress and ego are intrinsically linked. This is because when we think then feel that people and things *have to be a certain way,* and they're not—we stress.

If you think you need to get three things done before you leave your home and you rush to get them done, that likely creates stress. You are letting yourself be run by a belief that is undermining your health and state of mind. Why not pause and ask yourself if you can let go of one or two of the things until the right time after you return? It's not the end of the world if, for instance, dishes remain in the sink filled with water until you can attend to them in a good frame of mind. It's important to notice what feels good, what feels right. Value your equilibrium. That is being wise. That is helping to prepare the field of your spiritual foundation.

Your Spiritual Foundation

When your ego is not quiescent, your mind is on fire. To master increasingly challenging times, a spiritual foundation can be a vital resource. Contributing to and being in touch with your spiritual foundation can greatly assist you in gaining wisdom and mastering it daily. With a good spiritual foundation, you can more readily be drawn to your spiritual center and empower it each time you return to it.

Your spiritual center is the state of mind in which you are most calm, grounded, centered, relaxed, detached, harmonious, open, present, and on purpose. When you're at your spiritual center, you are least anxious, frustrated, scattered, agitated, tense, fearful, and focused on the future. Also, you are in some degree of control of your mind instead of your mind pulling you every which way by uncontrollable ego, greed, attachment, lust, and anger. Thus, your attention is centered. Your thoughts are not agitated. Until you are a saint, however, your mind can pull you every which way—usually away from your spiritual center.

Your actual, present spiritual center is the seat of your soul. It's a little above and between and *behind* your eyebrows. It's not a physical place. It is where your awareness is. When many people forget something and they are trying to remember, their fingertips automatically go to touch that place. Think of your spiritual center as the power and light arising from and energizing your spiritual foundation.

Good positive character is the ballast upon which the foundation of spirituality is built. They go hand in hand. Good positive thoughts are the outcome of a vital spiritual foundation. And yet, you are not your thoughts. If you've not pondered this and embraced it, now is a good time to entertain this key concept of spiritual growth.

You are the soul, that immortal particle of love energy and knowing that is connected to LoveSource, simply another name for God. The soul is being dominated by the mind until, through your spiritual progress, you master the mind and then it becomes your best friend. For now, the more you access and act from your aquifer of consciousness, the less likely you are to do things that do not serve you and are simply unwise.

Your kindness, love, intuition, and giving are what build your spiritual foundation. Giving is being of service to people, giving money to honest, worthy charitable causes, and giving of kindness and goodness to struggling souls—like yourself—with whom you come in contact.

Learning to live from your spiritual center, in your highest state of knowing, is a way of life you will love more and more. As you begin to live there, you will gain an appreciation of your higher mind.

Higher Mind, Nobler Mind, Better Mind

Our minds are a vast realm of worlds. The potential expressions of your mind in these coexisting worlds may be looked at as being on a continuum from lower mind to habitual mind to higher mind.

Higher mind, which you can call nobler mind or better mind, is that part of your mind that is positive and likes to be kind, benevolent, and of service. Your habitual mind is that part that assists you in getting on in everyday life. The habitual mind will make you get to work, take out the garbage week after week, brush your teeth. The lower mind is the mind that is a slave to your senses. It is apt to get lost in sensation, ignoring negative consequences. Think of people who enjoy spreading dirt about someone, enjoying someone's misfortunes, being mean—they are at the mercy of their lower mind.

Think of an eternal light bulb. That is your soul, pulsing with love for LoveSource. Now envision it with strips of gauze wrapped around it, then strips of cotton fabric, and finally strips of canvas encrusted with dirt covering all. The gauze represents your higher mind, the cotton your habitual mind, and the canvas your lower mind. You can find ways to clean the dirt and unwrap the canvas that is obscuring your better self.

You can also conceive of your mind as a vast sphere (or activity) with storms, surging seas, sultry winds, earthquakes, languorous breezes, typhoons, tornadoes, and quieting mists—mental that is. These mental expressions are active and dormant and, when triggered, they sweep across your consciousness. We are captives of our mind. We will remain subject to the whims and terrors of our thoughts and impulses until we are the true masters of our mind. Until then, we can begin, easy step by easy step, to further this evolution. For instance, you can begin to realize when your mind is streaming negative thoughts, but also that you don't have to listen to them. Further, you can begin to develop the knowing and power to replace those thoughts. The negative mind is a powerful foe that can ultimately become your best friend.

When the active sphere of your mind rises higher in consciousness, the lands and seas grow calmer, the climate and environs salubrious. When you prioritize spirituality, you can mine great riches: stalwartness, goodness, helpfulness, and more. Go higher and you realize empathy, giving, love, and a stronger connection to our universal Higher Power.

You are most at peace when your better self is predominant. Your better self is in the fore when your higher mind is dominant or, at the very least, when your lower mind is momentarily quiescent. Your better mind expresses itself as your well-wisher, your inner glad girl or boy, your sunny disposition, your good conscience, your nobler self, your innocent who wants the best for everyone. Your better self is your positive self. The more positive we are, the more fully human we are. We begin to recognize the inherent goodness in everyone and our connection. Realizing that many people act at the mercy of their minds, we are ready to forgive, let go, and move on in our own journey.

The Power and Rewards of Commitment and Engagement

Having a clearer understanding of your mind and how it can be both ally and saboteur in your realization of wisdom, you are better able to work with your mind. The more your higher mind is present and active, the better you are able to empower and access wisdom. Working with this book, the five phases of integration of wisdom into your life are: idea, belief, faith, practice, and conviction. Step by step, and returning to them step by step, you can make a profound commitment to lead your best life possible. You keep your commitment activated by returning to embrace the idea, shore up your belief, muster the faith to practice wisdom, and, seeing the changes, form and strengthen the conviction that you can master wisdom daily and return to a state of equilibrium. This is the engagement necessary for transformation.

The thirty-three wisdoms will give you ideas and directions of where to focus and exercise your awareness. When you are introduced to a wisdom and you embrace the idea that you can master it, you will shore up your belief that it can, in actuality, be mastered even when doubt or negativity billow in your mind. You will muster the faith that you already have the wisdom within you or that you can access the wisdom. Then you will practice this wisdom when situations arise in your life that call for it, or when you realize it is a good time to promote it. Thus, with your commitment, you will engage your mental and intuitive abilities, and these will evolve and strengthen as you continue to practice.

Commitment and engagement are keys to success. If you fail to make a commitment, you likely will fail to engage with the good practice you need and deserve. If you make a commitment, but it is vague, loose, or dishonest, you may engage with some of the practices once or twice and when things arise to divert your attention, your practice will fall by the wayside. Your journal can be an invaluable tool in supporting your commitment and engagement.

Believe that you know yourself best and that you know how to integrate new practices and awareness in your life. You have the ability to figure out what will work best for you to embark on the adventures ahead. This is using your intuition, your wisdom, to know what is the next best thing to do or way to be. The reward? A new life. A new now—now and now and now—with possibilities, opportunities, and riches now available to you. These treasures will give you gratitude and joy for a life that you truly love.

CHAPTER TWO

The Eleven Loving Wisdoms

The Wisdom of Humane Interactions
The Wisdom of Acceptance
The Wisdom of Being True to Yourself
The Wisdom of Grooming
The Wisdom of Thanking
The Wisdom of Commonality
The Wisdom of Fulfilling Friendships
The Wisdom of Attention
The Wisdom of Discipline
The Wisdom of Feeling Good
The Wisdom of Love

The Wisdom of Humane Interactions

Throughout the day, opportunities arise to interact with others humanely. Studies have shown that human interaction is the most important factor favoring longevity. But more important than simply logging years in this life is the quality of your life. When you finally leave, how many hearts will you have gladdened? How well will you have grown in love? Simply smiling when you cross someone's path or making friendly chitchat with a cashier or a waiter can uplift you and the other person. Particles of love are exchanged between you. Love is life.

When you are pulled from your mortal coil, what empathy will you have given to lighten another's load? Invisible but present is the spiritual juice that passes between you and another when you express yourself humanely, kindly.

Be aware. As you go about your day, nudge yourself out of your comfort zone and interact with people—who are all human beings like you. Don't overwhelm them with an outsize personality. Be natural. Interact with people appropriately with the awareness you can muster of who they are and where they're coming from, responding directly to them. Be positive, be kind, be cheerful—unless it feels dishonest.

Our culture is rife with insincerity. How often have so-called friends asked, "How are you?" and passed right by before you could answer? While it may be tempting to concoct a smart, sarcastic remark to hurl at their backs, why inject negativity? People are where they are, typically doing their best, however lacking that may appear. If someone seems to honestly ask, "How are you?" and you're going through really tough times, you don't have to put on a false smile and answer, "Great!" You can be positive and respond, "I'm doing as best as I can." If the person is sincerely interested in knowing more, you can summon your awareness to respond with the details that you feel they can handle, but that also honestly represent how you are doing.

What if you could *see God* in everyone?

Imagine this for a moment. If the soul is immortal, a shimmering particle of the Supreme Being, then everyone has—no, *is*—that indivisible, shining, loving element. Humans who are fully spiritually realized actually *see God* in everyone. That these humans are loving, compassionate, respectful, and peaceful reflects that.

Try this for a day or a week. Each time you see someone, imagine that you can see that person's living, loving soul essence. Regardless of what mood they're projecting or how you otherwise might feel about them, believe that the true person is their soul and you are connecting with it. This will spiritualize and elevate your humane interactions.

Webster's defines humane as "marked by compassion, sympathy, or consideration for other human beings or animals." Spiritually realized in this context means having achieved the awareness and inner vision (with subtle spiritual senses) to see and know that our true identity is soul and that our minds are not us; minds are for functioning in the mental and physical realms of existence. Being human is living in a physical world— in our case, Earth—while also possessing both the spark of God and the potential to master our minds and realize our divine birthright.

The Wisdom of Acceptance

The wisdom of acceptance is a wonderfully profound wisdom that the more you practice it, the better you will be able to reap the rewards of equilibrium and happiness. Other benefits are being in the present, peace of mind, and getting on with your life. We will touch on three spheres of the wisdom of acceptance: reality, people, and feelings.

When you lovingly accept reality, you finesse resistance. When you're resisting, you are stuck in a false reality. Accepting reality is not being passive. It is starting where things are and then deciding whether to rise above your nagging thoughts or whether you can work constructively to change the situation. An example is if your mind is railing against a path you've taken. It could be a career path, a relationship you got into or avoided, or a place you moved to. Thoughts besiege you: *If only I had... I wish I had let myself be interested... This place is too hot, too cold, too dull, too lonely.*

Why not accept that divine right action is taking place? Everything has happened for a purpose and it's all for your ultimate growth even if you don't see this now. If divine right action doesn't sit well with you, how about affirming the situation as follows? *It is the way it is and I allow myself to let go.* Or *I see the beauty in my life, I do my best, and I let it rest.* You can know what resonates well with you to transform your relationship to the reality nagging you. You can experiment with what resonates best by trying out affirmations or understandings of the situation, repeating or revisiting them throughout the day and then tuning in to how you feel about the situation. Can you let go of it? Can you feel okay about it? Can you feel that better opportunities may present themselves further along your path?

This can be the beginning of an adventure: learning how to work with your mind so that rather than resisting a reality that keeps you stuck, you make mental adjustments to progress in your life. This may mean taking an action or not. The focus is learning how to accept a reality you've been railing against so that you can establish your dynamic balance and get on with your life.

Another sphere in which we can be challenged to accept reality is people, specially their behavior, which can be difficult to accept. Pay attention and notice when your mind objects to someone's behavior in your thoughts and even in your speech—talking at that person or gossiping. You can't make people change. You can be an exemplar of good behavior and be loving. This projects positive energy that may inspire them to change on their own. If they don't, over a reasonable time, you may need to make a decision about your relationship with that person. You can try communicating your feelings honestly, humbly, and kindly. The situation may change or not. You can ask your higher self what is the best thing to do about the relationship, know how you feel as options present themselves, and act once you feel a positive confidence about the course that resonates best for you.

Harboring a love or physical interest is a situation in which it is easy to be delusional. For instance, you might believe that someone is truly interested in you and it's just that they're shy and afraid to show it. Observe the other person neutrally, especially their responses to what you say. If you feel it might help, make notes about "What's so." Note their responses to what you say, do, and what you may write. Do your best to understand the reality of this relationship and accept it.

Another common situation in which you may not accept the reality is with people who used to be in your life but have fallen away. Without inventing a reason of why this is so and latching onto it and feeling bad, simply accept that they're not available and let go. You can take reasonable steps to connect with them when it feels right, letting go of expectations. The opposite situation is when someone who is not the best person for you is attached to you and their presence is a bad influence or is dragging you down. Next time they call and expect to see you, you can say, "I'm sorry, but I'm not available." If they remain oblivious to your reality, you can always speak your truth, kindly. If it is someone who for now *is* in your life—a family member or a coworker, for instance—you can do your best to establish healthy boundaries and situations and play your role humanely while being detached and not compromising your better self.

The last thing we ever want to do is hurt someone's feelings. Intentionally hurting someone's feelings hacks away at your root of spirituality and is bad karma. There are ways to learn to communicate your truth so that someone gets it and, if their ego is in the right place, accepts your truth without taking offense and making you wrong. If their ego does flare up, making them say and do things that are unfortunate, you can speak your truth with love if you are so moved.

The vital flip side of this is to accept your feelings. You can barrel along in your life, pushing feelings out of the way, but feelings are important signals for what is going on, "what next" is best, how to be, where to go, which idea to develop, and more. If you're pushing away your feelings, you will miss these signals. Loving wisdom is to attend to your feelings and honor them, giving yourself the time and freedom to know what your feelings are telling or showing you.

The Wisdom of Being True to Yourself

Accepting your feelings is a key to being true to yourself, as well as loving yourself. By being true, you will spare yourself much grief and regret. To be true to yourself, you need to know yourself—that is, observe and know your feelings, affinities, aversions, strengths and weaknesses, and needs. Knowing this whole mélange of aspects of you can enable you to lead a balanced life.

One key to leading a balanced life is to be aware of yourself and notice when you're feeling off. Then tune in to feel and know what way or ways will rebalance your life. For instance, perhaps you've gone out five nights in a row. It might best serve you to take the next two nights to be at home luxuriously alone. Or perhaps for the past week and a half, you've watched shows every evening with your partner or alone. Might it be good to sense what might truly feed you and plan it? Perhaps it's dinner with a friend you haven't seen for a long while, or a hike, or bowling. Scan your feelings as you entertain different ideas.

You have physical, emotional, intellectual, and spiritual needs. Fulfilling one type of need that wants attention helps balance the others. When your favored activities get more of your time and become ever more comfortable, you may not try something else that is challenging but could nurture you. For many people, it's far easier to be passive than active. In this way, life—a new now—can pass you by. Don't forget—you are going to die. It could be when you are absolutely not ready. Now, you can summon the courage and will to discover what specifically would fulfill you so that you don't go through life and depart with unresolved desires and regrets.

Exercising the wisdom of being true to yourself is in your best interest. You may fail to make commitments due to fear. This may be precluding positive, growth-inducing engagements in your life. Oppositely, you may be overcommitted, spreading yourself over too many taxing commitments. These are examples in which knowing yourself well and using your wise discrimination will serve you as to whether and how to commit or what commitments to adjust. Be careful giving your word. Being true to yourself includes maintaining a wholesome integrity so that when you give your word and commit, you follow through. Keeping your commitments is powerful and sustaining.

Behaving in your best interest includes the important realization that you are a spiritual being. Being true to yourself in the way you think and act supports this. Your true self is your immortal soul. We are so fully our minds that consciousness of our souls and the soul's yearning is readily lost. But you have a specific spiritual purpose this lifetime, being here on Earth in the physical. You may not know it until this life is over. Wouldn't it be fascinating to explore what it might be?

Examples of spiritual purpose are:

❖ To express and enhance your higher nature through art
❖ To loosen the pulls of the world, to see and experience the emptiness of worldly ambition, and to form the desire to attain higher states of consciousness
❖ To realize that living things are alive and appreciate and

respect the essence of life, and to experience true longing for God

❖ To realize that everything we do in life matters and what matters most is the love and kindness we give to every living thing

As you progress through life, your awareness may grow to attain an appreciation of what is your spiritual purpose (or purposes) this lifetime. Regardless of how certain you are, you can align yourself with what you sense is your spiritual purpose, and devote yourself to fulfilling it. Then you can revisit this purpose when you feel an intuitive nudge, reaffirm it, modify it, or express an entirely new one that further honors who you are and your mission.

The wisdom of being true to yourself utilizes your higher sense of knowing to recognize opportunities for growth and take advantage of them. On the path of this lifetime, opportunities may be available throughout the day. When you are fully present, you can better recognize these opportunities, such as to be giving, to be loving, to be of service, and to stretch beyond your ego's selfish insistencies.

Experiences follow one after another, constantly. Your challenge is to act with an awareness that honors your self and to suss out what is actually true about the experiences. In this way, you accrue wisdom and then each time you engage—with people, your thoughts, your desires—you do so consciously with your growing wisdom that supports you in being your best, loving self. As you engage with experiences throughout the day with greater awareness, you are grooming yourself for a better life, a truer life, a life on a higher plane.

The Wisdom of Grooming

Different kinds of grooming can improve your life in key ways.
Grooming operates on three levels—physical, emotional/men-
tal, and spiritual—separately or together depending on what
you are grooming and your awareness. Grooming consists of
increasing and enhancing the cleanliness and attractiveness
of your appearance, removing inexpedient features from your
goal, and preparing for a specific objective.

Taking time to clean yourself with healthy products can be a
loving act. You can care about your appearance without inflat-
ing your ego. You've been given this physical body. It is changing and aging all the time. You can help it age in any number
of pleasing ways without harboring a negative complex about
how it's aging and how you look. When you groom yourself,
you are facing yourself with varying degrees of awareness. If
you have a negative reaction to a certain aspect of your appearance, that is self-defeating. It is like throwing a heavy, gloomy
shroud over your temple, which your body is. Thus, grooming
can also be transmuting or letting go of detrimental beliefs and
behavior patterns. If negative or judgmental thoughts come up,
you can tell your mind with strong intent: *My higher mind over-
rides down-pulling beliefs.*

Meanwhile, you can care for your body and take positive
steps to enhance your appearance using beneficial products that
you can afford. Cleaning your teeth. Taking a shower. Cleansing
your face. Applying cream that will protect your skin from the
sun. Massaging your scalp. Brushing your hair. Doing these

things, you can choose a positive attitude such as: *I am honoring this gift of a human body.*

If you view a physical feature as undesirable, it is a roadblock, interfering with or preventing you from fully realizing your objectives such as peace of mind, happiness, creating a harmonious space in which your life can unfold, and/or contributing the best way you can or making the most of your life. You may not be aware that you have created a roadblock, but it is a negative pattern that is ordering your life. The secret of physical grooming is that it is an opportunity to *love yourself.* It is taking a reasonable amount of time to take care of yourself, lovingly, and when you go out in the world, you present this loving self to others. This is a loving wisdom.

Your physical appearance changes day after day. This temple we've been given is for a limited time. Eventually—in thirty years, three years, or three days—you will give it up.

Whether or not you believe in reincarnation, it will happen. After you die, at some point your mind and soul will be stationed in another physical form. Why not seize the opportunity now to take charge of your destiny? You can decide what is your main priority and groom yourself for its realization. You basically have four choices:

1. Pursue your worldly desires and goals without regard to your coming fates.
2. Decide what you wish to achieve for the remainder of this life but also the next and work toward that end.
3. Decide you wish to do everything in your power so that after you die you are rewarded with a stay in a heaven.
4. Decide you wish to leave physical existence for good to

transcend all suffering and to realize increasingly spiritual states of soul liberation, bliss, knowing, and supreme love.

It is up to you. This is your chance to shower yourself with some critically crucial loving wisdom. If you believe in destiny, forget about it now and how a decision might affect how it manifests. Act as though you are a free agent with the free will and wisdom to groom your future as best you can.

Even though you might be so advanced spiritually that you know what good and bad karmic debts you've amassed, it is doubtful that you could know what destiny will be formed for your next life from your reserve of karmic debts. Yes, act as though you can create your destiny. To do that, you can forge a new now in which you are proceeding with cognizance toward your goal. Thus, committing to and following the second choice, you would knowingly groom yourself for the best life possible in this physical life and/or a next physical life and/or your ongoing spiritual life.

Perhaps you're a musician but only part-time because you've had to focus on your family and earning a living. When you least expect it, an ardent longing surfaces in which you feel pulled to create beautiful transcendent music. But time is limited. You're middle-aged and you have overriding responsibilities. As an example of the second choice, you can work toward this end as time naturally allows. Great opportunities can still open up that you never expected. For instance, you could receive a buyout from your employer and you could comfortably retire or get an easy part-time job for some flow of income while you pursue your music and composing in what is a new life.

If a big, unexpected break does not materialize, you can still enjoy your music and study composing when the times are right, as you harbor the deep desire to compose and contribute transcendent music. If you do this, there's a good chance your desire will congeal into a destiny that must be fulfilled. Your next human birth could have the most propitious circumstances for your development as a musician/composer. You might even develop key elements or abilities *between* physical lives. This is possible and, in your present realm of knowing, uncertain.

Perhaps, rather than harboring a grand overriding ambition, you want a break. You deserve a break. You've heard of heaven many a time—and most of these times, it sounded ridiculous. Still … you are intrigued. Many mystics have described the existence of heavens. There are a vast multitude of heavens. Wouldn't it be wonderful to live in a heaven on and on and on?

There is a way you can pursue that goal: by developing your life to do good works without the expectation of any reward. You will need to manage your ego well to keep it at bay and simply want to contribute to do good, truly to help people, to exalt the divine in everyone. Perhaps this has been your calling all along. Look over your life. Look at what may have been particularly heart-gladdening. A path may already exist to your new now of selfless giving. Yes, you simply need to explore and discover your true path.

Perhaps, you want the biggest break of all. You may have undergone an enormous amount of all kinds of suffering. You can see the suffering around you, all over the world. You desire an all-embracing love, forever. The uncertainty of life in this world is something you'd like to escape. If you believe in reincarnation, there's no knowing what gruesome acts you committed in past lives and how you might have to pay them off. In future lives. Even this one.

If the fourth choice is what truly resonates with you, then the adventure of your new now becomes particularly keen. Your goal then is to seek. Find and read books. Search for the right teacher who, after thorough research, you feel can guide you to everlasting liberation and bliss. Search on the internet, if and when you are so moved, using search phrases such as: "liberation of the soul," "path of eternal love," and "self-realization," "God-realization," or whatever you feel pulled to search for.

You are embarking on a sublime, soul-stirring, soul-empowering adventure. As you progress on your path, you will use your intuition and awareness to good effect and you will have much for which you can be thankful.

The Wisdom of Thanking

It is the tendency of many a mind to think about what it does not have instead of what it has been given.

If you pause for some moments and reflect on what you've been given, you can find much, for instance two legs and two arms that work, a place to sleep, sufficient clothes, enough money to buy food, a home, a voice, the ability to hear, a sense of right and wrong, a good heart.

Thanking is the signal way to express gratitude. With genuine positive feeling, you can thank verbally, mentally, or both simultaneously. A good heart is a grateful heart. Thanking connotes an inherent humility.

Sincere gratitude is God-appealing. Have you ever noticed

that when you expect something—especially when you think it is your due—it does not show up? When we don't hanker after what we don't have, we allow ourselves to receive just what we need. Be it something you're happy to receive or something you don't want to deal with—like throwing your back out—it is all part of your path. This is an opportunity to take better care of yourself—for instance, stretching and strengthening your core muscles on a regular basis. If you see health professionals, you won't know what you're meant to exchange with them. Perhaps you'll find yourself expressing grateful thanks to a physical therapist and that is pleasing to you both.

When you sincerely thank someone, a current of love passes between you. The other person feels your gratitude. True thanking is the rare, all-purpose, high-grade oil that makes the moving parts of life move better.

Each of us possesses a spark of the indwelling God. Even though you may not be fully aware of this, it is true. When you thank someone with a true heart and the other person receives your thanks, for a moment you're both encompassed in a bubble of communion. With this simple interchange of love, you are ennobled. Most of us are struggling in this world and trying to do our best. The humane aspirant expresses the wisdom of thanking, uplifting other and self in a spiral of love.

If someone thanks you and you toss off, "No worries," you are tossing their thanks back at them. You are rejecting the opportunity to receive and bask in that person's gratitude. If instead you look them in their eyes and express a sincere, "You are most welcome," then you are both uplifted and, in effect, you return the favor.

"Thank you" and "please" are three fundamental words with which we communicate. Those who are immune to their expression are failing to interact humanely. Those who think they don't need to thank are cutting themselves off from their Creator. Their humility is wanting. We are alone and yet we live in a community in which we all share the same, sacred essence of Life. Thanking someone is giving thanks for any service they have performed but also acknowledging that invisible mystical community of which we are part.

The Wisdom of Commonality

We live in a community of living beings—humans, other animals, birds, fish, insects, and plants. We also belong to various particular communities of people. These may include your blood relations, the property subdivision or complex in which you live, your city or unincorporated area, your state or province, your professional, artistic, athletic, hobby, spiritual, religious, and ethnic communities, your nation, and our planet.

You belong to acknowledged or undiscovered communities of one or more persons with whom you share a commonality of interest or talent. If you have an interest, talent, or good character trait, it is for a reason. Regard each as a gift. They are clues of who you are meant to be. Connecting with kindred spirits can further you on your journey. Regardless to what extent you have developed your talent or interest, when you get to know those who share your commonality, it is an opportunity to bond. By bonding and supporting one another, you can better capitalize on, enjoy, and develop your commonality.

If you are open to an adventure that will enliven and advance you, why not consciously choose to be with those persons with whom you can enjoy becoming geniuses together?

You may very well be a genius at one or more things. And your awareness of this can vary from being as yet unaware to having only glimpses of it, or to knowing you may be but feeling too shy or afraid or constrained to do anything about it, or to feeling in your heart of hearts that you are a genius at one special thing but so far have been unable to pursue and actualize it.

Webster's defines genius variously as "a strongly marked tendency, disposition, or flair of any kind; ... a strong leaning or inclination; ... a singular strongly marked capacity or aptitude; ... notable talent; ... extraordinary native intellectual power especially as manifested in unusual capacity for creative activity; ... transcendent mental superiority, inventiveness, and ability."

You can be a genius for being reliable, staying in touch, working with animals, teaching music to children, listening, finding the right healing treatments, or developing your intuition. In the days to come, ask your higher self if you are a genius. If you feel this is affirmed, continue to explore and ask to discover exactly what this is.

You are often most alive when you are grappling with the very stuff of life and empowering your wisdom in and through your unique gift, when you are practicing your genius. The person(s) you share your commonality with and with whom you can further develop your genius may be a peer, a mentor, a colleague, or a student. Through sharing experiences, learning, or mentoring, your genius is quickened. Be discerning. Rather than judging someone's status, select those persons with whom you feel an inner pull to be with, people who will further you on your path.

Even being with an acquaintance who is oblivious of your interest and heart's desire can be helpful when just being in their company helps you feel positive. If you happen to be on your own without the potential benefit of interaction with others who share your interest, you can seek companions in other commonalities as you deem appropriate, or simply be grateful for and exalt in the times in which you devote yourself to your interest or talent in glorious solitude.

Whenever you focus on expressing your genius, with others or alone, do so from a place of humility not ego, love not entitlement. Regardless of whether you identify with possessing a genius for something, developing your commonality with others is a loving wisdom because you are evolving the nascent you—becoming who you can be. Also, this enhances your appreciation of a shared humanity that is of a particular focus and expression. Moreover, when you share with people who seem different, to whom you could affix a whole set of labels different from your possible labels, in this diversity you experience a beneficent commonality. You are being fulfilled in something near and dear to you and in this you can create fulfilling friendships.

The Wisdom of Fulfilling Friendships

How does enjoying fulfilling friendships enhance equilibrium and the mastery of wisdom? Enjoying fulfilling friendships nourishes your humanity. These interactions allow you to express the best parts of you while, at the same time, taking you out of yourself—your small, querulous self. Fulfilling friendships balance you, helping to satisfy your human needs. Time spent *positively* with such a friend gladdens your heart, helps you feel lighter, and can flush out your negativity. Furthermore, a fulfilling friendship makes you part of the human family and your specific human family—that which you share with your friend.

A fulfilling friendship helps you to transcend your small self and experience something greater as you experience a type of union with your good friend. Care must be taken that it continues to be healthy and affirming and not based on toxic ego-stroking or gossip.

To enhance your quality of life and even your longevity, it is important to enjoy fulfilling friendships. According to a 2010 study conducted by Julianne Holt-Lunstad at Brigham Young University, the two strongest predictors of how long you'll live are close relationships and how much interaction you have with people throughout your day. And why not make them *humane* interactions? You can have contact throughout the day and be closed—not much more than a living automaton—and miss out on the benefit of humane interactions.

To be a fulfilling friendship, the relationship needs to fulfill you in at least one of these seven connections:

- Cultural—this includes sports, theater, movies, series you watch together, gardens, music, hobbies, and physical activities, like walking in neighborhoods, hiking in nature, or bird watching. When you genuinely enjoy watching or engaging in an activity in the company of a friend, then you're in your cultural element.

- Intellectual—engaging thoroughly in conversation with a friend and getting to the nub of a topic can also provide the basis for a fulfilling friendship. The topic or topics can be movies, sports, series, novels, sustainability, politics, orchids, or myriad other topics—even quantum physics.

- Emotional—you can nurture a friendship in which it is safe and customary to express your emotions to one another and experience empathy. This lightens the burden of whatever you're going through. This is different from being codependent when a so-called friend is encouraging or abetting self-destructive behavior. Here, the element of friendship is based on freely expressing feelings and empathy.

- Work—supportive, healthy friendships can flourish at work remotely or in person. For periods, you may spend more time with a coworker or a boss or an assistant than anyone else in your life. Particularly if you are devoting extra-long days to work and you work with people or have repeated contacts with those at another company or agency, you can develop a fulfilling relationship. The most successful enterprises are those in which all parties work together to perform their work well and support one another ethically. Thus, there is no gossip, undermining, negative politics, or sexual misconduct. It is a safe environment. With work friends, you don't need to share your innermost secrets. You don't want the relationship to devolve into bitch sessions or put-downs. You can model good, positive behavior by interacting and working together effectively, efficiently, positively, and with well-placed humor.

- Open—an open friendship is a safe relationship in which you feel comfortable and free to bring up just about anything without the fear of being judged. You respect one another. You have integrity and respect boundaries, which includes not divulging what the other shares without that person's express permission, and not gossiping. You treasure the friendship because you can communicate what's on your mind—no matter how seemingly mundane or trivial—and you feel like sharing it with this friend who will most likely appreciate it. You're not necessarily looking for justification—perhaps understanding and the occasional insight. If you have such an open relationship or can move a friendship into a truly open space, this is valuable and fulfilling.

- Spiritual—a supportive spiritual friendship in which judgments are absent is wonderful indeed. A fulfilling spiritual friendship supports you as you follow your spiritual path. It can be supportive by helping you deal with challenges; inspiring, when you discuss the teachings or read from texts; and beneficial, in helping to fulfill a human need so that you know you're not struggling alone to awaken further. It can assist you in moving forward when you are struggling. For instance, when you are assailed by doubt, experiencing difficulty in your spiritual practice, or trying to understand the spiritual benefit of what you are experiencing, your spiritual friend can help you restore clarity, confidence, courage, and more.

- Intimate—an intimate, fulfilling friendship is one in which you can share your innermost feelings, hopes, fears, and goals. It is a safe space, based on mutual trust and integrity. When you communicate and share intimacies, the person responds honestly, without judgment. It is different from what is termed an open friendship in that it is marked by and founded on closeness, depth, and highly personal details. If you are lucky to share an intimate friendship, this can be the most fulfilling. An intimate friendship can coexist with any of the other kinds of friendship, as can the others.

A spouse can embody one or all of these elements. Sometimes there is an element that can be discovered later in the relationship and added. For instance, finding a sport that you can enjoy together can bring many benefits, including strengthening of companionship and patience, improved communication, letting go of pride while engendering empathy and acceptance, a new element of harmony, and enhanced romance. Once you discover it and engage in it, this new interest can renew and enrich your relationship, creating an expanded reality.

The most fulfilling friendships are those in which you both are able fully to be yourselves and share genuine intimacy. If you are able to open up any of your existing friendships to include closeness and intimacy, that would be good and wise. That is because an intimate interaction with a close friend flushes away negativity and constraining feelings of aloneness, as well as nourishes your well-being.

If you feel that it would be wise to find new friends or to enhance existing relationships, do the following when the time feels right. Make a list of all the people you consider friends (including relatives), identify the main kind of connection (for example, cultural—you watch sports together), and here's the careful, important part: ask your higher knowing whether that friendship is fulfilling. If the friendship is fulfilling, you experience a fullness, an upliftment, or a true satisfaction after interacting with that person. This does not have to be every time you interact. If it is not, ask if it has the potential to be fulfilling. If so, do you want it to be fulfilling? If yes, wonder and intuit what you can do to move it into that zone. Write a plan with those relationships you intend to make more fulfilling and how that can be achieved. Also, if you'd like to create new fulfilling friendships, come to understand which activities you most enjoy and look for venues where you can meet those who share your interest. For instance, it could be a garden club, a book club, a dining group, or a walking group.

It takes commitment and engagement to create and maintain a fulfilling friendship. An important ingredient is taking the initiative to stay in touch and to get together. If one person is predominantly the passive partner, that creates an imbalance and the friendship can wither away. Unless you have an agreement in which one party confirms that they're too busy or shy or passive to initiate and asks the other to always take the initiative, then doubt may creep in the active party's mind as to what extent the other person truly values and wants the friendship. Reciprocity is always to be valued and encouraged. Reciprocity means *mutual* action, influence, or dependence. Reciprocity issues can arise from one person always initiating getting together, picking up the check (or not ever), or dominating the conversation. In many friendships people are reticent to discuss the relationship, particularly to address reciprocity if it is an issue. This is why, if you value the relationship and want to enrich it, you may want to bring up the issue, breaking through any resistance, in a non-accusatory, positive way.

Friendships can sour when one or both of you harbor doubts and perceived judgments that may have no basis in reality. Your thoughts can lead you astray. Communication is vital in a relationship. Communicating questions about aspects of your relationship may be painful or awkwardly difficult because it feels too personal and foreign. But love can be a function of communication. Do you want a mutually fulfilling friendship in which you thoroughly enjoy one another's company once or twice a month to devolve to the point where you see each other once or twice a year or, ultimately, not at all?

Ask yourself: What would loving wisdom do? Would your loving wisdom go out of your comfort zone to communicate with the person to know if you both would like to see more of each other? Or would your loving wisdom let you know to send your best to that person mentally and let go of the relationship?

As an expression of God, you have a responsibility to yourself to evolve as well as you can. Ultimately, this is what wisdom is about. Fulfilling friendships are valuable and needed experiences on your journey, but relationships are but one of the many focal points in your life. Where are you choosing to direct your attention? Attention is an energizing element of wisdom.

The Wisdom of Attention

Your attention is where you are. It's what you are conscious of. Your attention is your *most valuable resource*. The ability to direct attention consciously is a prime human attribute and power. You can develop your attention as you explore and practice keys to equilibrium and as you master wisdom daily. What hijacks your attention succeeds in frittering away your time. Your time is your *most precious commodity*. Therefore, ceding your time is giving up your life, particularly when you let your attention be hijacked by opposing forces.

Let's further explore what attention is. *Webster's* first defines attention as "the application of the mind to any thought or object or sense." It also can be defined as the process of focusing your consciousness to select your awareness and/or to enhance your perception. Let's look at it another way. The more you attend to something, the more you *become it*. When people fall in love—passionately, overwhelmingly, joyously—all they think about is the other person, visualizing them, conjuring smells and feelings, and to the extent that they forget themselves, they lose themselves in the other person and, in effect, become the other person.

In a profound sense, then, attention is what you love. For instance, if you love your football team, you will attend their games or watch them on television and read about them. How many parents would prefer not to sit through their child's games? Because they love their child, they attend the games to watch their child play. If you love yourself, you will attend to your needs—nutritional, spiritual, environmental, cognitive, directional. By cognitive is meant the process of acquiring knowledge and understanding through the senses, intuition, thought, and experience, which includes conscious experimentation in your awareness. A cognitive need would be the need to engage with and understand a book that you're reading. Directional refers to the areas of life you need to move toward and experience, like finding ways to have good fun, or be in nature and feel invigorated.

If you wish to practice and realize the wisdom of attention, look at where your attention is throughout the day. At the start of your day, coming out of subdued consciousness—sleep and dreams—of what are you aware? What do you first think about? And then and then? Problems you face at work? The disturbing things you watched last night on a show? Being aware of these thoughts and images, you may wish to let go of them. One way is to engage in repetition. For instance, you may wish to repeat a mantra you've created for yourself or been given that you fully trust. You may repeat a positive affirmation that you've come to feel is beneficial for this particular period.

In getting up and moving about in the morning, make yourself whole and right again. Take responsibility for finding and developing the best practices for you to start each day. It could be any of the following: stretching, drinking water, stepping outside and breathing fresh air, kissing your partner or yourself, yoga, meditation, feeling grateful for a new day or any of the myriad things for which you can be grateful. You may realize that checking the news, immersing yourself in the strife of the world, diminishes your focus, attention, and mood. Therefore, you may wish to choose your sources of news wisely, as well as the time or times you attend to them. If it is preferable, you may also choose to turn on your phone at a later, appointed time. *Don't let yourself be a slave to what demands your attention.*

Practicing and ultimately attaining the wisdom of attention

is *choosing* to what you attend. Be aware of thoughts, noises, mental and physical urges, what you look at, what you do, how you order time. *Be aware of what you are aware of.* While you do this, let your higher sense of knowing decide whether your particular thoughts and whatever is crossing your awareness are what is best for you to attend to. Then choose that which is best for you.

Opposing forces are constantly grabbing your attention and influencing your actions: competing thoughts, anxieties, fears; family, friends, and coworkers; a welter of emotions; news; desires that keep demanding their satisfaction. To experience a new reality, again and again throughout each day, gain the power of your attention to serve you in the best ways as you continue to master wisdom daily.

The Wisdom of Discipline

Practicing and attaining the wisdom of attention grows from commitment. Without commitment, the goal will wither and die. With commitment comes discipline. Without discipline, the competing demands that assail you each day will overrun your commitment, rendering it mere wishful thinking.

Discipline in this context means engaging in continued practice, training, or experience that corrects, molds, strengthens, and perfects. The word "discipline" originates from the Latin *disciplina,* which means "instruction" and derives from the root *discere,* which means "to learn." *Discipulus,* which means "disciple or pupil," also stems from *discere.* Thus, you will become

a pupil and disciple of your higher self and learn to love these
contacts.

As you practice mastering wisdom, you will learn to focus
on listening to your higher self. Great things are accomplished
with discipline. You can experience joy and renewal by following a discipline and returning to it again and again. In this way,
wisdom is accessed and informs your everyday consciousness
and life. In this way, it can expand and transform your life into
a wondrous adventure. Ultimately, following the disciplines
that open you more and more to higher knowing, your life can
become an engaging learning journey that whets your curiosity
and runs smoothly even when things seem to go wrong. And
if pain comes, you'll be better able to deal with it, summoning
compassion and also knowing to discover how to seek improvement as best you can.

Thus, as you tread your unique curious path, practicing the
mastery of wisdom daily, you are acting as a disciple of your
higher being, the being that ultimately can know all and act in
accordance with the highest will. Acting in accordance with
your highest will means you are empowering your higher mind,
which ultimately can become a trusted ally of your soul. The
main discipline you will follow is learning how to heighten
your attention.

For now, entertain the following qualities of evolved or higher
attention while harboring the faith that you can develop them.
Know that you can cultivate a compassionate detachment while
maintaining a steadiness of mind and a focus that is strong and
also relaxed. This, along with enhanced intuition, will lead to an
expanded awareness, a certainty as to what is true and knowing

what is next. As you work with yourself, strengthening your attention and expanding your awareness, you will be unexpectedly surprised by your evenness of mind, calmness of thoughts, and your ability to apply wisdom to your everyday life. It is thrilling to live on a higher plane. You might presently be a disciple of worry, hurry, scatter, and at times, the mad Hatter. Now, more than ever, in our crazy world, rising above the craziness ensures real benefits. To lead our best lives, we need to strive for equilibrium.

What are the keys for achieving equilibrium? The keys are what you teach yourself: they are mental disciplines, physical recreations, and emotional invigorations you incorporate when needed and appropriate so as to empower your nobler self by taking time to grasp and turn a particular key. Then you respond rather than react to thoughts and events that demand your attention. Remember, attention is your power, your *most valuable natural resource*, that, with practice, you can replenish and focus at will rather than letting it be hijacked by all the crazy and ordinary things that steal into your consciousness and run away with it.

For now, as you introduce the wisdom of discipline into your life, hold discipline as a gentle, forgiving father would hold the hand of his child who is learning to walk, with his other hand resting on the small of the child's back. At times, when it is safe and good to let the child walk on their own, the father will let go. If the child stumbles and falls, it is part of the discipline of learning to walk, then sprint, and eventually running steadily for long distances, avoiding pitfalls and perils along the way.

You can learn to summon lovingly the discipline needed

to engage with the practices in this book. Learning when and how to engender discipline calls for you to love yourself. Love yourself like the most attentive, patient father. Love yourself like the wisest guide. Imagine it—you can create a whole new relationship with yourself. If the idea of discipline is something you ordinarily would shirk from, know that discipline is simply continuing to show up and follow through on what you are committed to as best you can without criticizing or judging yourself. Yes, this is an opportunity to transform how you approach what you wish to achieve and how you nudge yourself. Mastering the loving wisdom of discipline will allow you to cover a lot of ground and discover yourself in new welcome places of being and expression, while feeling the good that comes from discipline.

The Wisdom of Feeling Good

Knowing how to feel good can optimize your self-directed evolving and facilitate your well-being and love of life.

How often do you sacrifice feeling good because you push yourself to do something? It may be that it doesn't need to be done just now, or you let yourself be deluded that this particular thing will make you feel good, when some aspect of your awareness knows this is not true. Our lower minds love repetition, addiction, misguided beliefs, and being out of control. Not feeling good can assuage guilt. Not feeling good can compensate for past commissions of hurtful acts.

Mastering the wisdom of feeling good as each day progresses from activity to mental state to activity while emotions and thoughts stream through you, always changing, will greatly assist you in mastering the other wisdoms. Learn to recognize how you feel when you feel good. It is a clean, clear, sober feeling. It is something that must be experienced and reexperienced to know what it is and facilitate returning to that state. Because it is a special and personal feeling, words can't adequately describe it. When you feel good, what you are feeling feels right, feels true, feels positive.

It is key for you to get wise to when you are not feeling good and take appropriate action. For instance, when facing a major (or a minor) decision, thinking through all the pros and cons, and what this friend said, what a professional said, you can get you more and more confused, and you may realize that you're not feeling good. You need to give yourself mental space, even physical space. You may wish to list the pros and cons as you see them. Then let go of them.

Give your sure, quiet voice the best conditions to express itself. If you can postpone it, let go of the need to make a decision. Engage in a physical activity that usually makes you feel good. It may be walking, gardening, washing the car, taking a bubble bath, going to a coffee shop and treating yourself to a mocha latte while reading a favorite magazine. Ideally, in its own time, a feeling of good will emerge around one of the possibilities in the decision you were contemplating. Along with this, there can be a feeling of certainty, confidence, or completeness. When in doubt, it's best not to act if what you are debating can be postponed. Remember, it may not be the optimal time to make a decision—you may still have feelings and thoughts to process, other experiences to live through.

You are given opportunities throughout the day to master the wisdom of feeling good. For instance, in the midst of doing something, you may become aware of a feeling that something is not right. Typically, we brush this aside. Learn to recognize when you are not feeling good and acknowledge it. Intuitive nudges often come when you least expect them and also when you most need them. The key is to attend to each nudge and explore what it is telling you. Discovering what that is and acting on it will deliver a state of feeling good.

An example of when you are being mentally besieged and would benefit greatly by activating the wisdom of feeling good is when a friend's negative, critical judgments are streaming through your thoughts every half minute. Often these are *imagined* judgments. Nothing has been communicated. Your friend may have taken an action or failed to, and now your mind is tripping on all kinds of judgments your friend has rendered about you.

This is an opportunity to exert your will, stop these thoughts each time they stream through, and repeat intently: *My higher mind overrules down-pulling beliefs*. Then get to the bottom of the down-pulling beliefs to dispel the thoughts that are making you feel bad. First, your belief is that your friend has made these judgments. Realize that you do not know what your friend thinks in this regard. What they did or did not do may be without a thought. Acknowledge that you are allowing your mind to buy into the down-pulling belief that your friend has made these judgments and replace them with what you know is true: *I honestly don't know what so-and-so thinks of me*. Then decide what appropriate action to take, if any. What will make you feel good? Initiating a non-threatening conversation with your friend? (Continue to toss out imagined critical thoughts as they come.) Allowing your friend to initiate contact when and if they do? Learn to test your options intuitively without allowing anger or ego to override your best intentions.

If a friend, parent, sibling, child, or anyone criticizes you (verbally or online), do your best to refrain from reacting negatively. View this as an opportunity to grow, to detach, to gain in wisdom. Rather than be defensive or self-reproachful or attack the other person, do your best to sense the nature of the criticism. If it is sincere and expressed in a spirit of helpfulness, then this can be an opportunity to adjust and improve yourself in a way that feels good.

If the criticism is, in fact, coming from that person's disgruntled feelings, their hurting ego, then it is likely all about them. Your challenge is to know the best way to respond. It may be expressing a simple, neutral statement like, "I've received your comment." And then refrain from getting into a discussion about it, particularly if part of you wants to make the other person see your point of view—what is "right." Even if what you can clarify is perfectly true, it won't be for the other person, as their reality likely won't allow it.

In the more fraught instance when someone confronts you in person, the stakes feel higher. Your challenge is to be calm, not swallow their energy and regurgitate it back to them, but to ask your higher self: *What would wisdom do?* Wisdom might do nothing. Wisdom might be aloof from the comment while you elicit love from your higher self. You can visualize that hurled remark as passing around you—so far that it can't affect you—and flying into the Arctic Ocean to be buried on its floor. You may come to know that the wisest course is to play a part—for instance, a loving, dutiful daughter because you know that the insult is merely an expression of your parent's unhappiness and doesn't mean anything. Further, the best course in this example—if it feels good—might be to suggest doing something your parent likes that will stimulate their happy attention. That can be an excellent mood changer.

For a major decision, such as moving to a new city, you may have tentatively decided on a particular city. You've been exploring neighborhoods, looking at lodging, attending events. You may be convinced that this is the right city for you, but where in the city is the right place? Doubts may be itching you. If you review your experiences and feelings and are aware of how you feel as you continue your exploration, you may realize that something feels off. You're not feeling good.

Perhaps then it might be best to postpone a decision and return to your home base, then patiently wait and see what is presented to you. When you least expect it, you may be presented with an option you'd never considered or an opportunity for a terrific work possibility, for example. As you explore the new option, delving into your prospective new place, you may find yourself simply feeling good. The wisdom here is to put aside preconceived ideas, recognize mental projections, and suspend judgments while you continue to test your possible new physical location. When your feelings about the new place reach a positive critical mass, then may be a good time to plan a trip to explore it.

As you further practice and experience feeling good, those

feelings may be enriched so that when you engage in some-thing—as simple as cleaning the kitchen or as unappealing as paying bills—you may feel a contentment, a love around you and in you. The wisdom of feeling good is a loving wisdom because you are proactively adjusting and experimenting with your mental, emotional, and physical experiences in order to take care of yourself knowingly, lovingly as the kindest of par-ents. You are elevating your consciousness in a way that you radiate love within yourself.

The Wisdom of Love

The greatest mystery is love. The greatest treasure is love. The greatest wisdom resides in and is expressed in love.

Becoming love is the ultimate realization, the completion of our spiritual journey to God.

Perfected love on this, our current physical plane of existence, speaks and acts automatically with the knowing of each per-son's needs and receptiveness. The wisdom of love starts with accepting then embracing that you are on a journey to becoming love—that is, if this is what you most want for your limited time in this body and beyond. Perhaps you are pulled to power, plea-sure, or pride. Then if you wish to live from a more enlightened place, your challenge is to pursue your pull with the wisdom of love.

Imagine the difference between the most enlightened, benev-olent ruler who is wholly dedicated to improving the lives of her people and a dictator who is consumed by being glori-fied and inflicting pain on his subjects. Imagine the difference between going on a weeklong, nonstop bender of drugs, sex, drink, and food, and using your wise discrimination to treat yourself judiciously to the precise pleasure you need now. After being acknowledged for good work, imagine the difference between responding with a sincere "Thank you" but also thanking all those who together made it possible, and stealing someone else's contribution to parade it around, feeling superior, to impress those you need to feel better than. Imagine the outcomes of these examples. Which cases exhibited loving wisdom, genuine caring? In which cases would the person feel wholeheartedly good?

While practicing the wisdom of feeling good, you may experience being in an atmosphere of love. Bask in that feeling. Learn to summon it within you and around you. Picture it any way you wish—perhaps you're inside an iridescent bubble of joy. Perhaps the air around you is charged with particles of rose and lavender scents that spiral around you. Going about your day at the right speed, with your attention focused, you can be in your own atmosphere of love.

You can enjoy and appreciate any love you feel from others, and that love awakens the love within you. If your inner self was a smartphone, you would not feel that love. Love comes from within. God, or LoveSource, is everywhere, including within you. During meditation, concentrating at your eye center (the seat of your soul between and behind your eyes) is the beginning of the journey to your third eye, the gateway to the realization of higher inner realms.

Loving consciousness is the wisdom to awaken to and learn. We are born to learn to love, to realize true love as best we can, *and* we have the opportunity to return to Love via the soul's realization of increasingly higher and purer states of consciousness. But we get lost in everything else; the mind loves its diversions, its immersions, its benders, all to forget the self, that spark of immortal love.

At times, the wisdom of love calls for discipline. It is summoning the knowing, the will, and the power to say, "No, thank you," and then engage with what truly feeds you. It may be doing "nothing." But by doing nothing, you can re-exist in your field of love, luxuriate in that uplift. From that, you may eventually come to know what is next. You can now regain your path, without second thoughts or judgment.

Endeavor to act with your best consciousness marshaled— that is, awareness that is attentive, loving, and discerning. If you feel unsure or stymied or feel an intuitive nudge to wait rather than act, pause and ask your higher self: *What would love do?* Then wait and allow that knowing to bloom in your consciousness.

Living in the wisdom of love is glorious. The small, ego-centered self is in retreat. You move through your life in an awakening field of benevolent intentions and sublime gratitude. You glorify God. As you do your best to glorify God, you find yourself thinking and acting automatically in a way that exemplifies being wise, furthering your evolution toward Love.

CHAPTER THREE

A New Vision

Terms and expressions that you've read so far may have been hard to understand, uncomfortably high-flown or ridiculously highfalutin, or seemingly too lofty to attain. You are simply being exposed to new expressions that, as you begin to live through your new experiences, will take on meaning, then more profound, lived-in meanings.

Remember, you can lead the best life possible for you. That is, a life in tune with who you are and who you can become. Hold this dearly in your heart. One way this best life can be furthered is by inspiration. You can inspire yourself by learning and practicing what you attend to in this book, and by living such an aware, available life that inspiration comes when you need it and you heed it.

No matter how difficult, dreary, or dangerous your life is, with the right positive attitude that you adjust as necessary, and by growing your wisdom, you can keep transitioning to the best life possible for you, a life that ultimately reaches your full potential. You don't necessarily know what challenges will come or what turns your path of life will take. Fixed ideas of where your path leads and who you are, what you should do, and what you should have are best entertained lightly. Let go of the hubris that you always know what's best for you, and also have faith that as your higher knowing develops you *will know* "what next" and what serves your nobler self best. You can create a new vision for yourself, your own personal, unique lodestar, and as changes come—relationships end, jobs end, your path shifts—your lodestar can take on different hues and your vision can be clarified, and then you'll see more clearly where you're headed.

One way to move toward creating the best life possible for yourself is by creating your own unique vision of that life. At a good time, ask yourself:

> ➢ What are my best qualities and feelings?
> ➢ What do I and would I most enjoy doing?
> ➢ When have I felt most alive?
> ➢ What awareness do I wish to attain?

Continue to explore what these questions elicit. Then, when you're moved to, write your answers in a place where you can find them, date your entry, and revisit it when the time is right.

Your new vision will come into better focus and realization as you develop practical wisdom day after day, experience after experience, and as you observe and tune in to your higher knowing. Don't look to other people for their advice, or worse, take their life as your own perceived trajectory. You are not them. You are potentially, if not already, the greatest authority on who you are and what's best for you. Each life is unique. Rise above external and internalized influences, peer and parental expectations, to chart your own course. Question your own expectations until you are assured and confident that they are authentic. Learn to release expectations grafted onto the true you. Be careful of expectations and attachments. Don't cling to them. View them lightly with a wry sense of humor.

Get in touch with what gives you joy, an inner thrill. Be attentive to what comes unbidden to you as an idea, a feeling, a knowing. Often an excellent way to encourage this is to walk alone in nature, clearing your mind of worries and occupations. What seems to be the next path or opening of your time on Earth? What gives you a tingle of excitement, a delicious trepidation, an automatic knowing that this is for you? Insights and inspiration may come when you take breaks after a period of focused concentration—for instance, while reading, you pause, gaze out, and enjoy a reverie.

As you evolve, remember what Epictetus wrote in *The Art of Living* after he was freed as a slave in the Roman Empire and became a philosopher: "Attach yourself to what is spiritually superior, regardless of what other people think or do. Hold to your true aspirations no matter what is going on around you." As you continue your journey of self-realization, it is helpful for you to continue to better understand who you are.

The Five Aspects of Who You Are

When you consider who you are, you may initially think about who you are in your first family and any subsequent family and also what you've gone through—major events, homes, illnesses, places you've lived. You may define yourself by your work—what you've done and achieved and the people you've interacted with. Part of your definition may come from those who have been influential in your life and the beliefs, practices, and characteristics you've allowed to meld into who you are. Your vision of who you are may involve your herstory/history of education, work, platonic and romantic relationships, and travel and your participation in athletics, avocations, mental preoccupations, and more. But who you are has different aspects and levels from what you might commonly think. To get a grasp of who you are that will enable you to engage with and understand yourself better, let's examine the five aspects of who you are. Here are the five aspects, each of which could have books written about them.

> Common
> Thinking
> Desirous
> Energetic
> Spiritual

The Common You

The common you is what you present to the world, what is recognized by the world, the so-called facts of your autobiography. It includes your appearance; your herstory/history with your family and relatives (the events and people in your life that shaped you); your herstory/history of education and work; familial, platonic, romantic, and animal relationships; and your participation in athletics, avocations, entertainment, and charitable, advocacy, and political organizations. Naming some of these items is how most people would commonly describe themselves if asked, "Who are you?" A profound and enlightening irony is that although you have your individual appearance, interests, stories, relationships, and personality, everyone else has all those, too, so we share this commonality.

The Thinking You

The thinking you is the world you inhabit with your thoughts. It's the busyness of your mind in terms of conscious, expressed thoughts, such as thoughts about an athletic game, a show, things to do at work and home, and family members. The thinking you subsumes your feelings, which you experience to varying degrees of awareness in your thoughts.

The subconscious thinking you is a universe of thoughts and impulses of which you are not aware. To some or a great extent you may be run by deeply ingrained, self-defeating subconscious beliefs that order your reality and defeat your best efforts to lead a happy life. Therapies can release these subconscious programs.

The Desirous You

You are also what you want. The desirous you includes thoughts and feelings about what you want. In learning to master wisdom and achieve equilibrium, you will need to examine who the desirous you is and how it functions. Desires, strong and subtle, occupy you, dominate you, and take you over, forming attachments. Attachments order your destiny in this life and your lives to follow. Thus, understanding the desirous you is a key to working with yourself and achieving the now that serves you.

As long as you have not mastered your mind, you are a slave to your desires. Some can be fulfilled easily. Others may take long, sustained effort and/or luck. Some may be beyond your gratification now, in several years, or perhaps later. An easy desire to fulfill, for instance, could be setting aside time today to meditate. This could have immediate consequences: while meditating, you could let go of stress or something important could dawn in your awareness. The more you are aware of the desires that preoccupy you, the more profound will be your understanding of who you are, who you may become, and how to work with yourself. Some desires that remain unfulfilled will form into karmas and be fulfilled in another life. Your desires impact the energetic you in ways you can discern and in ways that, for now, remain beyond your grasp.

The Energetic You

In addition to the observable and non-observable energetic interactions constantly taking place in your body on a phys-ical level, the energetic you is an amalgam of subtle energies. Some advanced yogis and mystics have seen the various sub-tle energetic centers, systems, and bodies of humans. These are called "subtle energy" because they vibrate and exist in finer and higher vibrational fields and thus are not readily seen in the physical. The following is merely to give you an idea and simple appreciation of the energetic you and is not meant to be an in-depth presentation.

Your physical body has six *chakras,* which is Sanskrit for centers, wheels, or circles. They are called: rectal (root), geni-tal (sacral), navel (solar plexus), heart, throat, and eye cen-ter. The first six chakras are reflections of the six centers in the astral realm, which are in turn reflections of the six centers in the mental causal realm and the pure spiritual realms beyond. Subtle life energy flows through these centers of the physical body fulfilling metabolic and systemic functions.

The sixth chakra at the eye center is where the meditator focuses their attention to withdraw their mind and soul currents to ascend to the third eye, the third chakra of the astral plane and the gateway to inner superconscious ascent to the regions of increasingly less and more refined matter, more mind, and more spirit. Attainment of the crown chakra, the fourth chakra of the astral plane (via meditation with the guidance of a realized Teacher) is the beholding and realization of the central powerhouse of the astral world.

You have seven energetic bodies that serve different purposes. These interconnected fields of energy vibrate at higher and higher rates in accord with their function. Briefly, these include your:

- ❖ **Etheric body**—your etheric body is an exact template of your physical body and holds the "blueprints" of your tissues, organs, muscles, and limbs. The etheric body vibrates at a slightly higher frequency than the physical body. Subtle life energy flows through the etheric body, providing order and organization for the physical body.
- ❖ **Align body**—your align body comes into being at birth and serves as a connection to your higher subtle bodies. It can be conceptualized as energetic connective tissue that aligns and integrates with the higher chakra systems. This second body or field is an integrative body that provides the potential for realizing aspects of your higher evolution because it is part and parcel of the

human miracle of the potential for spiritual evolution in consciousness that is largely hidden but possible to those residing in the physical.

❖ **Access body**—your third subtle body comes into being hours after birth, supports being in the physical by providing access to mystical powers of communication, and dissolves at death. The first of the two main powers of communication allows one to communicate directly with similarly advanced humans, but also with beings in the astral plane, the first grand division or plane of existence beyond the physical. Only at certain levels of consciousness can these powers of communication be accessed. The second of the two main powers allows one to communicate and understand automatically, transcending the need to articulate in language. When the access body is properly charged and the person's mental sphere sufficiently advanced, its energy fields enable these powers. Further, the person has the potential to realize and access other powers that can be exercised in the astral realms.

❖ **Etheric template body**—the etheric template body has the energetic building blocks of the lower etheric body and is the template that exists before the physical body is formed.

❖ **Astral body**—your astral body is your main body in the vast astral realms and is associated with your astral mind. Every person has and uses an astral body even if unaware of it. If you were able to see your subtle energetic astral body, you would be able to attain a greater and better appreciation of your mental-emotional states, especially as they change.

❖ **Lower causal body**—your causal body actually consists of a two-part energetic body: lower and higher. Both are present when traversing the lower causal realm (and are with you in the physical and astral worlds). In the vast, indescribable causal realm are two energy centers or chakras for the lower and higher causal realms, with the lower causal having a lesser admixture of spirit. The causal body is the soul's vehicle and means of communication in the causal realm.

❖ **Higher causal body**—when your mind and soul pass from the lower causal to the higher causal plane, the aspects of the lower causal subtle field dissolve, yet they are reconstituted when your mind-soul entity descends back to the lower causal plane. The higher causal plane is more refined and luminous than the lower causal realm and is the last plane with mental admixture before the purely spiritual realms.

The Spiritual You

The spiritual you includes impressions from past lives, your life between physical lives, and your innermost, true you—your soul. Your soul is the true spiritual you and ultimately who you are. The spiritual you is also your yearning for true love, the pangs of separation you feel for your true home, the wonder realm of pure bliss, surging love.

You Have an Unlimited Capacity for Growth

An important element of your new vision is gaining a fuller appreciation of your true potential. Your true potential is that you possess an unlimited capacity for growth, for expanded awareness, and for love. Each person's capacity for growth in their ability to understand life and how best to chart, steer, and allow their advancement through life is unlimited. With practice, and mastering wisdom daily, you can come to know what is truly for your good—and what is not. To think that your education or lack of it limits your ability to grow and to know is a fallacy that rejects your true potential. You have the potential to access inner resources of enhanced awareness.

Much time, precious time, is wasted doing things that are simply unnecessary. If they feed you, it's with empty calories. More and more, you can develop a higher knowing and let go of things that don't serve you, freeing yourself while still fulfilling your true responsibilities. Too many of us give up our knowing to what we think is a higher authority outside of us. Your ability to know is an innate ability. You can depend on yourself, discover how to teach yourself, and thereby gain true self-reliance, self-grounding, and self-knowledge.

As your discrimination increases as to what is true for you and what is best, you will come to realize and be confident that you are the best and ultimate authority of who you are, who you can become, what is true for you, what resonates, and what does not resonate with you. With your exercise of discrimination, you can learn to inspire and energize yourself and also come to know what you do love and bring that into your life. What you discover can renew and transform your life. As you work with this book, you will be teaching yourself how to achieve this and your higher purpose.

As you develop this innate capacity for knowing, your life will prosper with increased relaxation, acceptance, richness, kindness, and contentment. "Life is either a daring adventure or nothing," Helen Keller wrote, and she was blind and deaf. Your growing knowing, increasingly accessing your higher knowing and becoming the person you can be, will transform your life into a daring adventure.

You Have an Unlimited Capacity for Expanded Awareness

You may have some appreciation of how you've grown in your awareness over the years as you've observed experiences and the results of your actions and those of others. Awareness in this discussion can mean: vigilant perception, automatic knowing, and/or comprehensive understanding of what is true. We are aiming to expand our awareness, experience by experience, into a highly developed sense of knowing and intuition; that is, when needed, coming to direct knowing automatically, without rational thought and reliance on assumed external authorities.

This is not to dismiss the role of clear, logical reasoning and study. Reading and studying wherever your formal or self-education takes you is vital to assess and profit from the professed knowledge of others. As you read and study, there's a higher part of you, a *truth-knower,* that tests what comes into your consciousness as to whether it rings true. Consciousness can be likened to a muscle that must be exercised and nourished well. If you listen to or read junk info—negative, down-pulling information and information that purports to be true but isn't—you will get mind-washed each time you do until finally you are dyed in the color of that source.

If you wonder about the relationship between your mind and brain, regard your brain as a computer or smartphone and your mind as the operating system and data within that device. When the device breaks, all that data can be uploaded and then transferred to a new device. Thus, you are not born as a blank slate. Rather, you come into a new birth with an old mind that has an exceptionally unique array of impressions, predilections, native desires, enlightenment, and training.

Now, while you are alive, how can your awareness be expanded? There are three main beneficences that can expand your awareness and five practices that will support these main three and are invaluable in and of themselves. If you develop these five practices, your experience of living can be elevated, refined, revolutionized. You will find yourself again and again in a new now, feeling more alive and adept.

The Three Beneficences

The three beneficences that can expand your awareness are:

- ➤ Meditation
- ➤ Service
- ➤ Love

One reason they are called "beneficences" is that they are three states of active good; that is, they are good for you, specifically your mind and soul, and good for others. They can automatically expand your awareness as you immerse yourself in them, loosening, lessening, and losing your ego self. Thus, when you lose your ego-centered self for a time in meditation, in service, in love, your nobler self can unfurl its wings and rise. The three beneficences transpire through you; that is, they subsume, circumvent, or quell the ego. The beneficences of meditation, service, and love happen in spite of the ego, when you let go and they come through you.

Meditation

If you wish to adopt a regular meditation practice, it is good to make as thorough a search as possible and adopt that practice only when you feel it resonates with you and you experience a strong pull to adopt it irrespective of the influence of friends and any persuasion by those who practice it.

Meditation is the best antidote to ego. Ideally, it will enable you to lose yourself, suspending the onrushing stream of thoughts, as you experience a transcendent state of being (for whatever timeless moments you do) and realize a higher consciousness that is cleansing, uplifting, and transforming. A good morning meditation in which you sit with utter sincerity and your best humble effort (regardless of how scattered your mind may be) will enable you to go through the day with a taste of bliss, in a beautiful flow, being on purpose, getting tasks done easily, often automatically knowing "what next."

The ultimate vanquishing of ego and expansion of awareness can come through meditating on and immersing your attention, your spiritual senses of hearing and seeing, in the Word, the inner mystical Sound Current, what has been called different names by different Saints, Masters, and Adepts in all their various times and cultures. It is the celestial sound and light that issues from and leads back to the One, the original Source of all.

Even your initial, faint contact with the Sound Current can automatically expand your awareness. If you are moved to, search for a Teacher, a Guide, who teaches meditation on the Word, the Sound Current. Initiation and practice of this meditation can slowly and surely clean your vessel of your negative, down-pulling tendencies, while washing your consciousness more and more in the pure Love Current that emanates from the Source. The domination of the mind, particularly your lower, baser mind, lessens and lessens as spiritual strengths come to the fore. This is soul service, for you are awakening your soul to its all-loving Source.

Service

Since there is a spark of the Source in all living beings, there is much, much to be gained by performing service for others. In true selfless service, you are acting to serve others in loving kindness rather than in vainglory. In service, the ego can get slippery, hyperactive, "knowing better," assertive. Wanting acknowledgment for your good deeds and wanting to show people that you know the best way to do things are self-defeating in developing your capacity for love. Service done anonymously is a good way to develop love as long as you're not mining the ego satisfaction that you are performing service anonymously, thinking, "Aren't

I great?" or "Now I'm really growing in spirituality." Here the
ego is doing its job and will continue to do so.

Service or volunteer work is best performed with the intention and attitude of pleasing God, Higher Power, Source—
whichever reference suits you best. One way of expanding your
awareness is working in loving harmony with others to achieve
a beneficial goal. Immersing yourself in the work, you can find
yourself working in concert with those of like intention and
surprising yourselves by what is being readily achieved, for
you have joined in a greater good and with that comes greater
awareness. Imposing your ideas or persuading others that your
way is *the way* will stop the harmony and defeat the purpose.
That's ego feeling right and feeding itself. Kerfuffles may come,
easily and often. Regard them as an opportunity to listen, to rise
above ego, and to emphasize harmony and your group's larger
purpose.

Performing service on your own, alone, is a special gift, for
then you are free of negotiating the egos of others and free to
concentrate on the task that you transcend, and with grace, sur-
round yourself in a loving atmosphere of pleasing the One to
whom all thanks are due. When you are in that state, you will
find that the good work simply flows.

Spontaneous service can be when you spot someone struggling to cross a street, open a door, or find something. It is
observing a person (or animal) in need—a stranger or someone
you know—and you ask appropriately if you can help. These
opportunities are often given to you when you least expect
them. We are not here for our own aggrandizement. We're here
to help one another. If God is aware of everything happening

simultaneously (because that highest consciousness is in contact with or part of each life), then imagine the gift of piercing your mental bubble to be aware of those around you, especially those in need. By helping those in need, you can experience love.

Love

True love is the greatest beneficence. Love works seeming miracles, it vanquishes seemingly insurmountable barriers, it is the stuff of life, the best stuff. We are here to learn to love. By being loving and allowing love to be in you and come through you, your awareness shifts so that worries, tasks that need to get done, and issues of your life adjust to their true value. Now, that's being aware. When you let petty things fall away to focus on your perceived purpose and your goals, you can love your life more and clarify your vision of what you do with it. This will engender a stream of love throughout your days as an active good. Love helps with acceptance, especially of hard, painful times. You can find ways to love the hailstorms of your life. It takes a little creative, positive thinking (and perhaps practice), or it may simply come to you if you are doing your best to be loving, for along with that comes expanded awareness.

The Five Practices

The five practices you can adopt and modify as your awareness grows are:

> ➢ Clean your vessel.
> ➢ Develop your sense of knowing.

> ➤ Cultivate detachment.
> ➤ Be an observer.
> ➤ Be aware of and manage your ego.

You can attend to the five practices when you sense or know it is appropriate and the right time. Initially, you'll want to emphasize each practice (on its own or with others, depending on what you perceive as best) until you feel that it is sufficiently established in your awareness and integrated into your behavior. Also, in certain situations, you may find it best to engage actively in a practice because it will serve you well in that situation. For instance, when you're participating in a group project or volunteering at an organization, it would serve you to be highly aware of and manage your ego. When you attend a family gathering and know that some relationships are fraught, it would be wise to cultivate detachment, which will enable you to be lovingly supportive in a way that serves you as well as others.

Clean Your Vessel

Clean your vessel mainly means leading an honest and moral life. In your daily dealings, be fair and honest. Clean your vessel also includes having good intentions for yourself and others. For all of your relatives and adversaries, why not wish them happiness or joy? One of the trickiest challenges of clean your vessel is to cancel negative thoughts. Once you notice a negative thought (and it may have been a long-spouting oily gusher, running all through your lower mind, and you're only just now aware of it), think good, positive thoughts. If negative thoughts continue to rise up and overrule your efforts, concentrate with laser-like focus on your task at hand, or, if you are free to, read an uplifting book or watch a good comedy. Also, if you have a beneficial meditation or affirmation process or a process for reframing a negative thought, you can immerse your mind in that.

Develop Your Sense of Knowing

Developing your sense of knowing is best regarded as a life-time practice. It will prove helpful throughout your life in many ways and become your trusted inner friend as your awareness and mastery grow. You develop your sense of knowing through study, intuition, experience, discrimination, and learning. You can gather and study information, using your sense of discrimination as to what is true and useful. When an inner prompting piques your curiosity, you can study the subject to the extent that this serves you. You can also study how your life unfolds throughout the day and season and benefit from this. You can intuit "what next" and, when glimmers of feeling or thought come through your awareness, you can intuit what they are. You can experience how you feel and what works best. You can also discriminate whether something or someone is good for you, and whether your current activity or path is beneficial.

Your sense of knowing can be developed further by learning—that is, by practicing, noting results, making corrections, reviewing and remembering what works, and integrating that into your life.

As your sense of knowing grows, you will increasingly be able to access it. When you are unsure about something, a good path to the best decision is to access your intuition or determine whether you need to gather more information to clarify the issue. The best decision may be to postpone the decision. Practice any of these aspects of your sense of knowing when you are prompted to. Those prompts will be your sense of knowing nudging you to utilize this greater awareness rather than impulsively lurching into an action or blindly following someone's opinion.

Cultivate Detachment

Cultivating detachment may strike you as being cold, unfeeling, not engaged, or closed down, but it is none of these. Detachment is freeing. It enables you to avoid being overrun by misguided emotions. It enables you to see situations and people more clearly. So easily do we get stuck in grooves of belief that our minds keep playing the same old tune, when a person or a job may have materially changed and we've failed to notice it. Banish expectations. Expectations are the enemy of living freely, automatically in an elevated sphere. Learn to discern between expectations and intuitions that come unbidden or you simply know. An excellent way to cultivate detachment is to become attached to something higher, like your ongoing spiritual evolution.

Be an Observer

Being an observer can help you detach from getting caught up in and unaware of the play around you. Rather than charging into scenes, with your speech issuing forth uncontrollably, you can choose what you will say. This can help you avoid adversely affecting your relations with others in confrontations, help you discover the intentions of others, and save you from some of the muck you may pick up as you go about your daily life. Being an observer, you can see how the other actors in the drama irresistibly and powerlessly stick to their script ("script" is used here to emphasize not being free to choose speech and behavior). They react, rather than respond. Be aware of how people interact, their body language, and what their eyes are communicating. You can begin to better understand people and situations through your higher sense of knowing. People can say one thing and mean something quite different. This is why it's beneficial to be able to read the person, the whole person. As you continue to observe people, you can appreciate better that most people are at the mercy of their minds, often their lower minds. They're being driven by desires that they are powerless to stand up to and thwart, release, or overcome. Thus, principles, morals, feelings, common sense, and goodness can readily be mowed over.

Be Aware of and Manage Your Ego

Be aware of and manage your ego, for ego is the enemy of genuine awareness. Ego is restriction, subjectivity, grasping needs, clinging to the past, obsessing with the future, fear, duality, illusionary elusive power, and parading dressed-up wisdom that is actually naked nescience. Being aware of your actions and those of others, see ego at work. Your ego can overpower and overshadow your better self. Observe the distinctiveness of your ego and that of others—how egos are self-aggrandizing, sly, pushy, tricky, and sticky. The ego can believe itself a genie that rises out of its lamp at will, expanding to its full power, believing it can make its every wish come true. What can best help subdue,

refine, and transcend your ego are the three beneficences: meditation, service, and love.

You Have an Unlimited Capacity for Love

The essence of your being is love. Pure love. Love that is free of
ego, of grasping desires, and disregard for living beings. This
love that is you knows the love that resides in all other beings
regardless of how it is hidden by negative mental wrappings
around your or their love essence. Your true being is soul, soul
that is the same as all other souls. If we can name a quality of the
soul, then it is love, pure love.

What is love? Saints describe it as losing your self in another
being; that is, your small self has been released and your true
self, your soul, merges in another being. When you are being
loving and giving, you're leaving your small self behind and
becoming to some extent the greater Self, that Self that is superconscious, fully cognizant of its connection to Higher Power, to
Oversoul. Because your actual life is due to the spark of the Self
within you, you are connected to that Higher Power. That is
your connection to Higher Power. Call it what you wish, that
Power, that LoveSource has no name. As part of the LoveSource,
you have an unlimited capacity for love. It's a matter of realization. Self-realization is when you transcend the mind to experience and realize that you are part and parcel of the Oversoul,
while the ultimate realization of the spiritual journey is losing
yourself, merging in the Supreme Being.

No matter how much love you think you can imagine, the
love you can ultimately experience is far beyond that. We could

call it the fullest loving radiance of the soul, though it is not truly communicable in words. This love is the realization of the fullest potential of your self whose essence is the pure love that *becomes* your consciousness.

Here, on Earth, you can develop love through the three beneficences: meditation, service, and being your best self to grow in love. Each small step and good intention is to your credit. Growing in love is done by loving thoughts and actions that are selfless, without ego-driven motive, as in simply being kind, helping someone, being nonviolent in every action. What gets in the way of developing and expanding that selfless love is your negative tendencies. Your lower mind wants what it wants. It, in turn, is driven by your senses. The mind is a great power that dominates the soul. The more you purify the mind, the more your higher mind, your better mind, gains the upper hand in thoughts and actions, and your soul becomes freer and shines forth with greater brilliance.

To gain a better understanding and a new and fuller vision of the facets of your awareness, exploring cognizance now and as you practice mastering wisdom will prove invaluable.

Cognizance

Your growing appreciation of all the facets of cognizance will enhance your new vision of who you are and further your evolution into the best you that you can be. Cognizance is having knowledge of something, conscious perception, and also the range of apprehension that you have. Seven facets of cognizance are:

- **Sense awareness**—perception of sensations, information, signals, and experience through sight, hearing, smell, taste, touch, and also the internal sensations of hunger, thirst, gastrointestinal perceptions (such as digestion and gas), heart activity, breathing, bladder and rectum fullness and elimination, blood sugar awareness, effects of drugs, and mental fogs and lack of clarity. There is also the perception of temperature, pain, body movement, body position, posture, acceleration, and balance. Humans also possess the soul's senses or powers of hearing and seeing mystical sounds and sights, which are awakened and empowered through contact with the inner Sound Current at your third eye.

- **Feeling**—an awareness and appreciation of your feelings. The degree of cognizance varies greatly from person to person and can also vary greatly within you. For instance, if someone you esteem highly says something that hurts you, you might bury the hurt and be only somewhat aware that something is off. Alternatively, if a close friend relates how a relative bad-mouthed them, you may experience strong feelings of empathy and, being aware of them, express these feelings to your friend. A different example is when a coworker you have mixed feelings about says something that fails to meet your expectations and you rush to regard it as a hurt, hold it as a prize, and parade it around, deriving ego confirmation. On the other hand, if a relative mentions that they really appreciate what you did for another relative, you might feel shy, a warm heart, and, simply saying, "Thank you," feel strong kinship.

- **Orientation**—awareness of yourself in regard to time,

physical location, compass direction you're facing, and your relation to living beings and non-living things. Examples of orientation cognizance would be your awareness that the time is almost noon, a dusty wind has begun to gust outside, and your cat has entered the room behind you.

- **Individuality**—awareness of aspects of your personhood. Examples of this cognizance would include awareness of the obvious, distinctive, and subtle aspects of who you are that differentiates you from others. Examples of these aspects are being an attentive, excellent listener; knowing when you need to take time out for yourself and doing so; and knowing whether someone is genuinely happy. Awareness of your personhood would also include a full appreciation of your personal characteristics, be they your ongoing loss of hair or the sound of your laugh.

- **Consciousness of others**—your cognizance of how others are aware of you. This includes their range of reactions and responses to your speech, actions, and presence. It can also extend to grasping what they are thinking and feeling about you. This cognizance can assist you greatly in getting on in the world—in your work, your family, and all your social circles.

- **Responsibility**—a mature grasp of your responsibilities and obligations in your various roles, including an appreciation of the benefits in fulfilling the responsibilities and the downsides of not meeting them.

- **Directional**—cognizance of where you are headed mentally and in life in an immediate sense and a much broader sense. For instance, if you are allowing negative thoughts to

inundate you, you are heading into a funk. If you are sharing more and more time with someone, you are entering or
expanding a relationship that will affect your life in particular ways and it would serve you to grasp intuitively what
these may be.

Developing these facets of cognizance as you go through
your life and integrating them into your everyday active awareness will add to your wisdom and your ability to master wisdom. Still, things happen. You get upset. Thoughts course
through you. Emotions wash over you. Aches come. Pains persist. You don't feel right, balanced, at peace. A good term for this
is disequilibrium. If you practice and master the keys to gaining
equilibrium, the quality of your life can improve immeasurably.
Being in equilibrium facilitates your mastery of wisdom and
confers many invaluable existential benefits.

Developing the facets of cognizance so that you recognize
when and how you are in disequilibrium and then taking the
appropriate steps to return to equilibrium is a great boon you
can work toward. Utilize your evolving facets of cognizance to
recognize when you experience disequilibrium, and then you
can come to know what to do and how to restore equilibrium.
Practicing this again and again will help you become a virtuoso
at your life.

CHAPTER FOUR

The Ten Keys to Achieving Equilibrium

The First Five Keys

Trust Your Better Self
Prioritize Your Day
Adopt a Positive Attitude
Learn to Know Yourself
Eliminate Unnecessaries

Trust Your Better Self

We are living in a welter of warring impulses. Our drives, desires, demons, and demigods vie for dominance in our minds. One moment you're longing to feel that you matter. The next, you want ice cream! But then that worry haunts you again about your health. You dive back into what you were doing but then … ah, you're lost in a fantasy with a demigod (or an acceptable approximation). Then your phone demands your attention— you need to make an important decision. What to do?

The first key to achieving equilibrium is to trust your better self. What will help you notably to get in touch with and learn to trust your better self is a quiescent mind. That's what we're aiming for. Rather than being bombarded by thoughts, a mind marked by the quality of repose and tranquility is one that assists you to be in equilibrium. That, in turn, can empower you to make the best, informed decisions.

What is your better self? How do you know you are presently being your better self? Your better self is when you are feeling and being positive, centered, whole, self-reliant, peaceful, kind, and/or confident. Naturally, the extent and expression of these qualities varies at any given moment. Further, it is good to appreciate that the path of your evolution unfolds over your lifetime and beyond. Acceptance, curiosity, love, and self-forgiveness will make a difference on this journey.

Here are two steps for getting in touch with your better self:

1. Return to your spiritual center.
2. Feel and affirm that you are pursuing your best purpose.

Spiritual center was discussed in "Your Spiritual Foundation" in Chapter One. Finding and confirming the best ways to return to your spiritual center and then practicing them is a wonderful goal and process whenever you notice that you are feeling the need—even a little off. This will help you be your better self and could even lead to discovering something about yourself. One of these three simple processes can help you return to your spiritual center:

• Perform a repetitive motion you enjoy.
• Sit or lie comfortably and take a mini mind-vacation.

- Sing, drum, or dance.

While you do the process, repeat a mental repetition or prayer, think positive thoughts, or evoke beautiful feelings. A good example of a repetitive motion is taking a walk, letting your arms swing comfortably, enjoying appealing, positive visual stimuli. Other examples are cleaning, swimming, knitting, and weight training. If you feel more drawn to restoring balance by being stationary, take a mini mind-vacation. Physically let go and take a mental trip to your favorite beach or mountain getaway. Summon the sights, sounds, smells, and feelings of being there. To enhance the experience, you may wish to listen to gentle music that inspires you or sounds of surf or the rain forest. You might also light scented candles or incense or diffuse essential oils.

When you catch yourself away from your spiritual center, take the next opportunity to practice one of these processes, the one that you sense will be most effective in releasing warring thoughts and return you to your better self. When you feel that you have returned to your spiritual center—or as close to being there as you can presently be—focus on and affirm that you are pursuing your best purpose. Your best purpose can be for your life, this day, or a particular project. It is invaluable to know what your best purpose is this lifetime. You can always reenvision it as you evolve, and this can serve as your life's lodestar because when you are not pursuing your best purpose as well as you can, you are not realizing the best you that you can be and become.

Your best purpose for this life is like a mission statement. If you don't know what your best lifetime purpose is, it may come to you or emerge while or after you practice returning to your spiritual center. Also, if you are moved to, you may find it by clustering. To cluster, take a sheet of blank or lined paper and with a pen write "My best purpose this lifetime" and circle it. Or if it feels better, you could write instead, "My best purpose this season." Choose a favorite color that lets you feel good. Studies have shown that for some people the color blue boosts creativity and opens the mind to new ideas. Now, mentally ask your better self: *What is my best purpose this spring?* Write the next thing that comes to mind by first drawing a line or spoke from the central circle, then writing the word or words, and circling them. If it's a whole line of words, you may want to write one word, circle it, a few small ones and circle them (with a line connecting the last circle), and so on. This is your creative canvas. When a new feeling or thought comes, see if you can intuit ideas, words, the truth of what you are seeking. When a new line of thought comes, it can work well to start a new spoke from the central question, continuing this line of discovery as you see fit, doing your best to articulate the exact words that express your higher knowing. If you feel that the truth of your best purpose eludes you, cluster anew when the spirit moves.

Examples of a best purpose this lifetime might be: self-realization; to explore spirituality; to experience the best the world has to offer; to further the education of young people; to be a good mother; to feel good about myself; to live in love. As you become better acquainted with what it's like when you are your better self, you can learn to trust your better self, rather than your limiting lower selves or people who may not know what is good for you. You have a well of knowing within you that you can access again and again. This will help with making the best decisions, taking the best actions, and simply moving through life as easily and effectively as you can.

Be wary of your thoughts. Your mind isn't always your best friend. Until we are saints, we are captives of our minds. We will remain subject to the whims and terrors of our thoughts and impulses until we are the true masters of our minds. Until then, we can begin, easy step by easy step, to further this evolution.

Like a dandelion seed, we are blown this way and that by the currents of our thoughts. Think of your thoughts as the dandelion seed's filaments that, caught by the wind, can send the seed anywhere, seemingly defying physics. The seed may eventually land on a rock and get parched by the sun, never to sprout. Think of the seed as your center, your *potential,* and the filaments as thoughts that *generate* the winds and breezes that fly the seed every which way. Stormy thoughts may whoosh it around and around. Depressive thoughts may belt it to the ground. Mean words by others may make it collapse in a pond, to be drowned. We are at the mercy of our thoughts and how people—especially close ones—act toward us, causing more and more thoughts to gust through our awareness.

If only we could mobilize and keep returning to our better selves, we would find that we are like a seed of a fruit tree that is unique, beyond ancient. The seed is your precious opportunity this lifetime to grow into a magnificent tree and draw on the accumulated experiences and wisdom of prior existences. If we find a fertile place to rest and root, we could grow in our own way, at our own rate toward the light, sprouting buds and leaves, drawing up water and nourishment, taking in the best of life around us to realize our own true potential, ultimately flowering and bearing fruit.

To become who you are meant to be, without being blown away to wither or root in an unforgiving place—a soil that does not contain the nutrients you need and want to facilitate your unique realization—you need keys to achieving equilibrium. As you practice and master more of these, you will find yourself enjoying a revolution in your being and your ability to negotiate what now in your life.

Prioritize Your Day

Have you ever considered how different your life might be if you were a master of time? This doesn't mean being able to stop time or go back in time. It means being able to flow through each day intuitively, automatically, knowingly so you make best use of your time, accomplishing what you'd like to at the optimal time when all the factors—your disposition, readiness, and confidence, but also any other person's availability and disposition—are primed for the task, call, meeting, business, or whatever else you need to attend to. Planning your day intuitively, using your best sense of knowing, and prioritizing what you do today and what you do another day will help establish and sustain your equilibrium and also make you more efficient and effective than if you had succumbed to what you wanted to lose yourself in online or to inopportune calls you took rather than letting them go to voicemail. You can move toward achieving prioritization along with a wise regard of your emotions, and this will further your sense of knowing along with your sense of time and your mastership of time.

Stages of Mastership of Time

1. Recognize that time is fleeting and an illusion and a precious gift.
2. Know that being caught up in time is a way to keep you from your priorities, your true life.
3. Check your mental impulses to act impulsively because something is roiling you mentally, or you're obsessing over it, and distinguish this from involuntary inner promptings.
4. Do things at the optimal time. Learn to know intuitively when the time is right to take action and when it is right to abstain from action.
5. Liberation of the soul from the mind and time itself.

To help you prioritize your day and focus on what is truly important, you may want to develop and write down your main priorities for the remainder of your life. Here are some examples:

- Health (including exercise, eating well)
- Family (including pets)
- Work

  Or perhaps:

- Living in the moment
- Eating less and eating more nutritious, appealing food
- Expanding my awareness
- Contributing my spare time to good causes

Or perhaps:

- Healing from emotional / sexual abuse
- Being in nature
- Supporting and enjoying supportive friends
- Finding and being in a loving partnership

Or perhaps:

- Loving and turning to God, meditation
- Health
- Family, friends, being a good human
- Work
- Service, giving

Or perhaps:

- Being positive and grateful
- Participating in a rich social life
- Learning something new regularly
- Reading
- Leading a balanced life

Within this framework, you can chart your specific quarterly priorities for spring, summer, autumn, and winter or any time periods that work best for the cycles of your life. The object is to be at the center of your life, attuned to a growing degree to your higher knowing, rather than merely being at the effect of things that happen in your life, being passive, and, for example, always waiting for friends to call you rather than calling them.

Within the framework of your life priorities and your quarterly priorities, you can learn to prioritize your day, so that it passes efficiently, effectively, and as consciously as possible, *and* you are progressing toward your goals. As you work on prioritizing each new day, learn what you do best when. And be flexible to changing what you do at what time, when your higher knowing prompts you.

It is important to write down your priorities rather than just keep them in your head. The point is to free yourself from unnecessary recurring thoughts so you can better focus on your task at hand but also recognize flashes of ideas and creative impulses as they come through and realize them more consciously before they flit away, possibly forever. Choose an organizer system that seems to fit your situation, or design your own form. It is preferable to write your priorities using cursive handwriting rather than typing or printing.

Studies have explored and confirmed that neural pathways and brain activity are activated while drawing out letters by hand but not during typing or printing. Handwriting requires far more complex motor skills and mobilizes far more muscles than typing. For children, writing by hand is a key step in cognitive development. Writing by hand is a boon to creativity and exploring your thoughts in a way that is better connected to your innermost feelings. Many authors do their best writing by starting with at least a first draft that is handwritten. Some of the most accomplished people keep a notebook handy. Advantages of writing by hand are that it can capture ideas, spark creativity, express your deepest feelings, and refine thoughts. Writing your goals and enthusiasms make them more real, tangible, and seemingly more attainable. It's a wonderful path from your mind through your brain and body to the pen and paper, drawing and enjoying the formation of the letters, and your sight of your writing, especially if it is in a color you love.

You may find that prioritizing your day (and writing in a notebook or journal) is far more inviting, effective, and rewarding when you write by hand, preferably in a beautiful color to which you are drawn. When choosing a color—and this can change day to day—the feeling or quality you would like when you write with the color is one or more of the following:

- A welcome invitation
- Opportunity
- Creativity
- Possibility
- Adventure

Entertaining such feelings or qualities as you write and forecast your existence for this gift of a day can enhance what comes through to help make this the best day ever. That includes your good handling of upsets and disappointments, which are opportunities to cultivate detachment and adjustment.

Other advantages of writing down your day's tasks and priorities (in addition to not having to keep remembering them) are that it helps you make best use of your day and enjoy a sense of accomplishment when you complete a task and check it off. On the page, it's good to separate major tasks from shorter ones such as responding to emails. Unless your job requires responding to emails as they're received, responding to emails is best done all at once when taking a break from higher priorities. This will enable you to maintain your focus and concentration. As to texts and calls, use your discrimination. Don't be at their mercy.

Plan your day when you are most energized to do so: with your morning coffee, smoothie, or tea; right after breakfast; first thing at work; planning your next day before you stop work; or after a walk or run when things you'd best attend to bubble through to your awareness. The main thing is not to feel overwhelmed or a weight by entering what to do. Prioritizing your day should feel freeing. One purpose is to free you of the mental cogitation of "What should I do?" Your daily plan is not carved in a precious stone—being in your new now will allow you to be aware of and act on intuitive nudges but also respond knowingly to unplanned contacts and events.

You might have resistance to planning your day, but once you do, you'll likely feel less anxious and more empowered to focus on what you need and want to achieve. Writing down the day's major and minor tasks assists you in getting things done that might otherwise be forgotten, which can easily happen when unforeseen situations demand your attention. Entering your priorities—staking your intention for how the day is to unfold—is also asserting your will over others' demands, although you will continue to need to discriminate what takes priority when something unexpected arises: for instance, a minor crisis at your child's school; your boss giving you a deadline; or a plumbing emergency.

As to how you prioritize what you list—for example, assigning numbers in the order you wish to complete your tasks, or placing asterisks before key tasks—this is an individual matter and depends on many elements. Rather than assign numbers as the priorities of the things you want to do, the order (and area on the page) where you place them may be sufficient. You

may want to buy or create a form with different sections for
main tasks and short emails, calls, and errands. A grid of hours,
divided into quarter hours, may be helpful for blocking in meetings, appointments, and key tasks. It's important to enter more
priorities than work and family duties, such as stretching, yoga,
going for a walk, calling a good friend with whom you haven't
been in touch, and stepping outside to enjoy the air and practice
the art of doing nothing.

A great idea is to enter a mental or spiritual state as a day's
focus. For example, be grateful, be carefree, pause to take deep
breaths. You may even enjoy naming the days before you enter
their date to set a mood or a theme. For example, Thankful
Thursday, Freeing Friday, Satisfying Saturday, Soulful Sunday,
Merciful Monday, Task-full Tuesday, Wonderful Wednesday.

The idea of prioritizing your day is not to give you a new
drudgery, but to empower you to complete and accomplish
what you need and want to and also make room for the things
you dream about that you always seem to put off then remember at unexpected moments before they again slip out of your
present awareness. Life is fleeting. Why operate at the effect of
what's happening around you and your own mental programs
when you can clarify just what you want your life to be and
align with and facilitate that?

Each day *is* a gift. A day is like a new life. A fresh start to make
your life anew. To grow in who you are meant to be and become.
Why do many novels and movies that are or are attempting to
be inspiring utilize *carpe diem*? That's Latin variously translated
as: "seize the day," "enjoy the day," or "make use of the day."
Unless you do, your day will flitter away in some game that

greedily chomps away at your hours, in pursuing conspiracy theories online, in fantasizing, in gambling, in checking your phone constantly, in being sucked into videos, in attending to unnecessary notifications, or any number of activities. Then, those precious minutes, that time is gone, forever.

After you prioritize your day, depending on your energetic makeup, it's usually best to start with that which is most important and/or difficult. That way what is most important gets done and not forgotten or pushed back again to another day because something louder or easier or more seductive took its place. Completing the most important item(s) first feels good and lets you feel lighter and enriched in different ways. Regardless of whether you prioritize and plan your day by writing, before you begin your planned activities why not first attend to that which you most highly value? That could be expressing love to your partner or child, practicing devotion to God or Higher Power, or naming and feeling gratitude for much in your life each morning when you awake—whatever you can summon in your awareness.

This is all empowering. As you practice prioritizing your day and adjusting, fine-tuning, and discovering what works best for you, equilibrium will rise and suffuse your life so that what matters gets handled and handled well. The steps and practice you take to prioritize your day are mastering wisdom daily. This is mastering wisdom daily because:

➢ You are mastering how to successfully handle competing demands.

➢ You are focusing your attention to achieve optimal and benevolent outcomes.

➢   You are recognizing and expressing what in your life is
     truly important; thus, your attention and actions reflect
     your values and goals—what matters wholeheartedly.

Adopt a Positive Attitude

To achieve your benevolent ongoing equilibrium, find which
keys you already possess and discover new keys to open your
thoughts and feelings to adopt a positive attitude. Be vigilant
when your thoughts and feelings go negative and then exert
your will and knowing to choose keys that will transform your
mood and thoughts to readopt a positive attitude.

Each of our minds has its own negative thought patterns.
Some of us tend to let our minds run frequent negative thoughts,
while others may be mainly positive and perhaps mask negative thoughts by various strategies of which they are unaware.
The challenge is to start observing your thinking and begin to
cease your identification with your thoughts. You are not your
thoughts, yet they exert tremendous, often overwhelming
power over every aspect of your life. The trap that's easy to get
caught in is identifying with your negative thoughts—believing
them, giving them power, becoming subservient to them.

Suggesting that you adopt a positive attitude—and readopt a
positive attitude when you notice that your thinking has turned
negative—does not mean that you adopt a falsely, blindly optimistic, unrealistic, untrue personality. It means being who you
are and evolving toward becoming a more positive being. The
more positive we are, the more we are fully realized human
beings.

While the mind can be a wonderful, helpful friend at work and with friends and family members when you are kind and helpful, it can also be your worst foe—sly, nefarious, sneaky, rationalizing, railroading, lying, clinging, sabotaging, counter-productive, destructive, wallowing in pity, and enjoying suf-fering—others' and your own. Why do people act hurtfully toward others, causing suffering? It is the negative mind, the lower mind acting out its negative passions.

An external source or strategy for adopting a positive atti-tude—if it works for you—is listening to particular music, play-ing a solo game, watching comedy, doing sudoku, whatever mood enhancers with which you interact that are by definition external. The idea is to derail you from the negative track and lift you into something you enjoy. Does the external source take you away from yourself and even mask what might be nagging you? Or during your interaction, do you adjust your attitude so that it is positive? Some people can switch to a positive attitude when they imbibe alcoholic drinks or eat sweet or salty foods. But aren't these a crutch? And to what extent do they compro-mise clarity of mind or mask why you are generating a negative attitude? Enjoying certain drinks and food in moderation while engendering positive feelings and thoughts may at times be an appropriate strategy, but does losing yourself in them take you closer or further away from your true self? Isn't the switch to a positive attitude actually taking place in your mind? Wouldn't you be more powerful, more effective, if you could adopt a pos-itive attitude on your own, internally, at will?

Rather than rely on external strategies or sources, it is more effective and transformative to develop inner resources to adopt a positive attitude. It's ultimately better to work with yourself, learning what works when. Start with the idea that you can become your own philosopher. A philosopher is a lover of wisdom. That is what you are and wisdom is what you are mastering. In addition to getting to know and trust your better self, get to know your cantankerous self, your frustrated self, your anxious self, your uncertain self, and your immature self. These selves are all expressions of your lower, negative mind.

When you notice your positive attitude has gone away, pause when it's a good time to do so and ask: *What is my attitude? What thoughts are making me feel down?* Perhaps you've been worrying that you won't be able to live the life for which you've been longing. Specifically, your worries may be about not visiting a place you've been wanting to experience; or that your life will be cut short by a heart attack, or you'll suffer an agonizing end with cancer; or unexpected expenses will devour your savings and you'll have to move somewhere you don't want to; or those you love will get busier and busier and have less and less time for you. In these examples, your anxious self is expressing the attitude of worry.

Negative thought patterns can be so ingrained that after readopting a positive attitude, when you think you're back on a positive track, negative thoughts shoot out again and again and take you down. Mental tapes may be running in the background of your mind and you may not even be conscious of them. The true key—particularly for ingrained negative thought patterns arising from subconscious sabotaging beliefs—may be finding the best process for releasing them. Efficacious therapies and meditations can help you release negative thought patterns. This may be something you decide to research and explore.

Being in the present, you can acknowledge that these are simply negative thoughts your mind is shooting out, like flares to get your attention. Rather than suffer these continuing bursts of worry, trust your better self. Believe that you can take positive steps to handle the root of the issue as best you can and move toward its benevolent resolution. To do so takes practice, as well as learning to know yourself, which will be explored next, as the fourth key to achieving equilibrium.

Learn to Know Yourself

If you are going to become adept at achieving and returning to equilibrium, it is important to know yourself. The implications of truly knowing yourself are profound. The main ones are:

- ❖ Being able to know your mind
- ❖ Being able to know what to do, how to be, and how to return to equilibrium
- ❖ Being able to realize that you are a spiritual being on a soul journey with a mind

This is an evolving process that can progress over your entire lifetime and enrich your life, bringing you purpose, fascination, ease, and wisdom.

❖ Learn to Know Your Mind

Three main focuses should enable you to know your mind. The first is: observe your thoughts. What are your recurring thoughts?

What dredges up the composting past? What thoughts herald a dubious future? How do particular thoughts affect you? Which thoughts help you establish a positive attitude?

The second focus is: observe what your mind performs best when. When are you sharpest? This can be the ideal time to schedule your most difficult tasks and projects. What brings up the greatest resistance? Perhaps it is paying bills or trying to understand medical bills or performing chores like ironing or cleaning. If these are tasks that need to be done regularly, such as weekly, pick a day and time when you are agreeable and relaxed for tackling them. Perhaps Tuesday afternoon is an ideal time for paying bills. If so, afterwards or on Wednesday, schedule something you particularly enjoy. If you hate ironing or stretching, rather than postponing it, having it come up again and again and drag on you, do it during an easy time and play music or watch a show you can listen to and look at occasionally.

The third focus is: observe what your mind loves to work on. This may reveal a unique flair or genius for what you can achieve and contribute, affording you deep satisfaction and contentment. If you are curious about this and nothing comes to mind, skim the past to find that which gave you an inner thrill, a taste of bliss. This is a key to what your mental self excels at and perhaps is your worldly purpose.

❖ Learn to Know What to Do, How to Be, and How to Return to Equilibrium

Being able to know what to do when and how to be are fruits of mastering wisdom. This is an ongoing process, explored at various points in the book, with a particular focus in "The

Wisdom of Attending to Intuition" and "The Wisdom of Asking Questions" in Chapter Five.

You're probably busy. Or you have all the time in the world to give yourself to whatever grabs you. You have too, too much to do, or you act as though time doesn't exist (and if it does, you've let yourself be convinced that it's not running out). Please don't allow yourself to be bamboozled by the programs of your mind, the illegitimate claims of others, and the mental viruses you've picked up along the way. As you work on yourself with the benefit of this book and your other studies, you will be priming yourself to know what to do, how to be, and how to return to equilibrium when you are out of sorts.

As you begin to master these wisdoms, more and more your life here in the physical transforms into a smoothly functioning, grand adventure. This is an adventure in which you learn to cope well with boredom, to deal as best you can with pains and difficult people, and to meet each challenge with trusty self-reliance. For now, before you set out to do something, or when you are unsure as to what to do next, or you have so much to do that you don't know where to begin, ask your higher self: *Dear higher self, what is the next, best thing for me to do?* Or ask God (*Dear God*) or higher consciousness—whatever feels like the most elevated, strongest connection.

As you transition through all the various bits of the day, ask your higher self: *Dear higher self, what is the best way for me to be?* Perhaps it is to be calm or determined or focused or optimistic or any one of these qualities: grateful, at ease, truthful, steadfast, or self-reliant. If you find yourself far away from or out of sync with your preferred state of being, then look at and intuit the best way to return to equilibrium and practice it. As you continue to know yourself better, you will have an effective arsenal of ways to return to equilibrium. Being in equilibrium, you can be, more and more, your nobler self.

❖ Learn to Realize That You Are a Spiritual Being on a Soul Journey with a Mind

A great, almost insurmountable challenge is realizing that layers and layers of wool have been pulled over our eyes—that is, our minds habitually spin thoughts that are woven into false realities that shield our spiritual eye. If the eye were to open, we'd realize that we are spiritual beings having a human experience on a soul journey with a mind. Coming to know yourself, is realizing that your self is a soul, a being of pure love that is subject to the drives and whims of your mind. This mind of yours can be your worst enemy or your best friend, depending on where it takes you.

Why are you here? Do you have a purpose? You are here this lifetime with a specific spiritual purpose. Your higher self, your higher mind, knows what your spiritual purpose is. This is a key element in that great ongoing school called "life," or better called "temporary existence in the material world." You may not realize it presently, but you experience life after life after life after life. Some human beings may be on their last life or are just here for a particular purpose and then may sojourn in a heaven, a higher, more spiritual plane of existence. We are supremely lucky to be human, yet many of us are capable of committing actions that will jettison our next human birth. If you do this, next time in the physical you will be an animal or, if you committed egregious evil acts, be consigned to a state of reformation—a custom-made hell.

Actions have consequences. The cliché "What goes around comes around" is true. It's just that you won't usually see it in your lifetime. Rare is the person who can actually see the inner workings of the law of cause and effect, of karma. If you don't believe in the law of karma, still, you can act as if it is the ruling principle of our world. What would it hurt? What effort would it summon? How might it transform your existence to an increasingly auspicious life? That's the opportunity of living more consciously and part of the reward of living nobly. To take the high road, especially when the supposedly justifiable temptation is to go for the jugular. To expand your consciousness to experience empathy and get a sense of what the other is going through. To adopt and express politesse, the forgotten virtue of social interaction. This is to be aware, as much as possible, of others' feelings, to know that we're all struggling, regardless of how we succumb to negativity; still, to speak with care and consideration and tact, even to offer positive support. That is a gift. For then you value the spark of divine within everyone. Thus, you comport yourself with grace. *Webster's* definition of grace is: "disposition to kindness, favor, clemency, or compassion : benign goodwill." This is not blind, false, or empty behavior—it's developing an awareness of the character and feelings of others and thinking and acting with that higher awareness so as to not injure the other, but rather to offer kind support, your better self.

Learning to know yourself is important in this regard. Observe yourself and notice when your dark side comes out. The serpent of ego likes to strike. Your ego may, at times, weave a web, a trap to ensnare friends about whom you harbor a grudge. We are the star of our universe, but that is but one among nearly infinite universes. You are special *and* you have an ego that is not to be trusted. Many extol pride as important, as an indispensable virtue. But "pride goeth before a fall." God inspires great works through the humble.

Knowing yourself includes learning your negative thoughts, bad moods, small feelings, pity parties, ego trips, grand ill-advised adventures, and sly insinuations. Once you recognize and acknowledge them, and learn what best dissolves them, do that, and then reestablish a positive attitude and love yourself a little more. You have shined a light in one of your darkened rooms and done a bit of cleaning.

We all have goodness within and express it at times. Energizing your positive self is a key to living in contentment and realization. The realization will come if you follow your own personal lodestar. It's a question of practice, of filtering out external influences and the demands of your ego, and being present in your new now to know your priorities each day, each hour, and the priorities (being and doing) that are allowing the realization of your new vision. In moving toward what you envision, what is inspiring and ennobling, and what will help you fulfill your purpose, you may struggle with competing priorities and all that is sucking up your time. There's another key for neutralizing this disequilibrium.

Eliminate Unnecessaries

Now that you are learning to truly know yourself, you can begin to focus on what you do each day and realize what is of value, what is necessary, and what is unnecessary. Once you do this, you can marshal your will to eliminate the unnecessaries in your life. This will help you streamline your life and devote yourself wholeheartedly to what matters. One liberating aspect of learning to know your better self and your priorities is that you can accomplish this life-cleaning. Our lives are cluttered with things and consumed by activities that are unnecessary. These keep us from that which would nourish us. We're constantly surrendering to distractions—exhibit A: our phone.

Develop an Awareness

For the next week, develop an awareness of how you spend your time. Notice the attention you give to things in your life and things you want. Refrain from making judgments. Make any notes you're moved to record. The following week, as you go about your day, question what is necessary and unnecessary. Ask your higher self: *Is this necessary? Is this?* When you feel positive and confident that something is unnecessary, eliminate it. Look at what facilitates and what interferes with keeping you in a state of dynamic balance. Remember, you are not a human doing. As you go about this, you can remind yourself that life is precious and ask yourself: *Why am I spending so much of my precious time on unnecessaries?*

After an intense day of work or with your children, you might wish to let go and zone out by watching some "comfort TV."

Ask your higher self and know whether this is helping restore you to your dynamic balance, your equilibrium. Also, be aware of the question of balance and avoidance. How much comfort TV are you watching? Is it so much that you never spend enriching time with that most valuable person—yourself? Perhaps taking a walk in nature would put you in touch with yourself. Are you ignoring other things, like tasks you need to get out of the way or richer time doing something creative or contributing to a good cause?

What about persons you value? Recall who they are. When was the last time you connected well? Are you zoning them out to a no-call zone or a no-see zone? When was the last time you initiated contact? You can determine the optimal amount of time for entertainment. Since most of us watch entertainment on devices that can be stopped and returned to at will, you won't miss out. Rather, you can enjoy the escape for as long as it is optimal and then attend to your responsibilities and make time to do what feeds and enlivens you more. And when a person you value who has been absent from your life surfaces in your awareness, can you break through any resistance to initiate contact and enjoy a humane interaction?

Discover and Learn Your Desire Minds

Since we're learning to achieve an ongoing state of equilibrium, a dynamic balance, learning how to work with your different "desire minds" is important. Most of us inhabit a wide spectrum of desires from wanting to contribute, to having mind-blowing sex, to giving back in a certain way, to fantasizing about giving someone a piece of our mind, to receiving an unexpected inheritance, to being on a secluded beach watching the light dazzle on the waves rolling in. We're not the master of our desires. They're the master of us.

For the next few days, notice your desires. Make mental notes and even try knowing "which desire mind" gives rise to each desire. You may want to cluster about your desire minds.

On a piece of paper, write "My prominent desire minds" and draw a circle around it. Ask your higher consciousness: *How many prominent desire minds do I have?* Likely, a number will come to you. Perhaps it will be seven. Write it down and draw a circle around it and a line from your central circle. Now, continue to ask: *Dear higher consciousness, what are my prominent desire minds?* When something comes to you, write it down and draw a circle around it and a line from the central circle. Perhaps your seven will include some of these: eating, watching, sleeping, reading, exercising, expressing myself, meditating. When one of these comes up, if you have a definite feeling that it's true, then likely it is one of your prominent desire minds. If you feel uncertain or if you want to confirm it (as well as you can), for each one you name ask your higher consciousness: *Is _____ a desire mind of mine?* If yes, put a checkmark inside its circle.

Study your desire minds. Ask yourself: *Am I spending too much time fulfilling the desires of one of these desire minds?* If you get a no, then you may be leading a balanced life. If you get a yes, perhaps you are spending too much time watching and eating. Study your desire minds in relation to how you've been spending your days. Maybe you've been eating too much, while starving "expressing myself." How much watching is necessary and good? Is your time and attention devoted to social media excessive, robbing you of social uplift and spiritual connection? Might you rebalance yourself and return to equilibrium by having a good talk, a humane interaction, with someone with whom you enjoy excellent communication?

How many days do you have left to live? You may think in terms of years—for instance, forty more. Or your dying may never rise to consciousness. If it does, you may bury this awareness with one of your effective escapes. Which desire mind or minds then spring into action? Regardless, you still have X number of days left. It might be 3,987, 676, or 79. Remember, when you are prioritizing your day you may be moved to *carpe diem*. Here then are opportunities to keep you on track. As you engage in your priorities and complete one and move to another, your desire minds will sidetrack you. These moments when your higher will is being hijacked are when you can learn to muster your will and eliminate those ensorceling unnecessaries.

Teach Yourself How to Master Your Will

You may encounter a lot of resistance when trying to muster your will to do something, and if it's a responsibility you'd prefer to avoid, you may experience such extreme resistance that your mind ably buries it time after time. Do you still want to make each day the best it can be? Do you want to continue to have things weighing on you when you could feel light and dynamic? What about responsibilities to others as well as yourself that you would admit are best fulfilled? When there are things you want or need to do that you're avoiding, you may be losing yourself in welcome interruptions, enticing diversions, or flights of fancy. Do you like the idea of the seconds in the sandglass of your lifespan steadily slipping away while you are shortchanging your inherent power and higher will? Might it be a worthy idea and need to figure out and teach yourself how to muster your will?

As to resistance, it is important to discern whether it is the kind of resistance that your lazy, pleasure-loving mind is throwing out, or whether the resistance is nudges from your intuition that there's something else you need to attend to and this is not the optimal time for what you were making yourself do. Now, decide on one or two things for which you would like to master your will. Is it overeating? Being a slave to your news feed? Backbiting or negative gossip? Putting off work or important chores? Adopt or adapt one of the plans that follow or create your own means of exercising your will. You know yourself, *and* you have the creative power to discover the best method or practice to reign in your self-defeating impulses.

Overeating: If you have a desire—sudden or escalating—to eat potato chips, chocolate, or ice cream, ask your higher self: *Is it sufficiently healthy for me to eat _____ today?* If yes, then: *Is it wise?* If yes, then: *What is the best time?* Perhaps it is with lunch or as a dinner dessert, rather than between meals. Then, at the right time, dish out small portions until you have the feeling that the amount is just right, or complete, being no more or less than what is best now. Then, if it is chips, neatly fold down the bag, attach a chip clip to it, and put it away. Or put the lid on the ice cream and put it back in the freezer. Or wrap the chocolate, place it in a baggie, and put it away. Did you hope to eat the entire large bar, but after asking how many squares of chocolate to eat, only two squares came up, but then unaware of what you were doing, you ate square after square? If so, the next time you affirm how many squares, put the rest back out of sight and leave it there until the next time.

At the appropriate time, *enjoy* your treat. Moderate amounts can satisfy you entirely if eaten with your good attention. Now, here comes a greater test: you may have a growing urge to take out the food again and help yourself forgetfully to more. Resist it. Muster your will and exercise that power. If the desire rears its head and nags on you, with your energized will say no and find a pleasant occupation to take your attention, detaching it from your focus on the food and attaching it to something that will feed you another way. (How about a written or verbal diary entry about what's circulating in your mind?) With a little practice, you'll soon forget about the food.

Device slavery: If you find yourself spending too much time on social media, a dating app, a pornography site, or playing games, you can teach yourself moderation and freedom from the device. First, determine what is the appropriate amount of time you can spend on a particular site that might humanely enrich your day. You may sincerely want to date someone and not merely swipe through the faces and bodies. In this example, determine the best time to do this: perhaps it's after dinner, rather than six minutes after you've started work. Once you've determined the optimal time to attend to this part of your device, once that time arrives, set a timer. Ask yourself what is the optimal time. A number will come up in your awareness. Feel whether this is the optimal amount of time for this particular day. Be it forty-five minutes or fifteen, set a timer. Once it dings, leave the app or the site and, this is where your test of will comes in, *resist* the urge to return no matter how empty, bored, or anxious you may feel. You can respond to messages when you know it is the optimal time.

Backbiting: Many of us want to share, seek agreement, settle a score, receive positive reinforcement. Any of these impulses can easily lead to tearing into a person once you've got a sympathetic ear or a captive one on which to unload. It's called backbiting for a reason: by saying mean things about someone, or negatively skewing events, or by making judgments about someone without acknowledging that you don't know the whole picture, it's as if you are sinking fangs and claws into that person's back and tearing out a piece of them. Regardless of the misguided payoff or perverse pleasure you're receiving, realize that you're dragging yourself down. You are besmirching yourself, empowering your lower impulses, impeding your spiritual evolution. When you're talking or texting a favorite fellow gossiper, resolve to steer the conversation away from negativity. If you're mainly on the receiving end, think about what would be the most effective proposal when your friend is tearing apart a mutual friend or stranger. Interrupt that friend. Introduce an entirely new, positive topic. If they revert to their backbiting despite your attempts at transforming the conversation into positive territory, decide whether to share your truth nonjudgmentally and possibly include it with an ultimatum to cease and desist the bad-mouthing or you might choose to end that relationship.

Postponing work: The best way to exercise your will to tackle work or chores you'd prefer to avoid is to schedule it on your day planner or calendar and when the time comes, be focused and tackle it with the requisite concentration. If it's a seemingly difficult project at work, the best time may be right after you arrive, or once you check and take care of anything requiring your immediate attention. If it's something that's best done with a relaxed mind, perhaps the best time for you might be late morning or midafternoon after you've attended to the messages and interruptions that have required your attention during the day.

Regardless of how often you feel you fail in these exercises, you are not failing, you are actually moving forward toward your goal. Thus, practicing mastering your will, regardless of how often you fail, will empower you, your higher self, and infuse you with positive conviction that you are moving forward to achieving your best life.

After eliminating unnecessaries and indulging your favorite indulgences with newly established moderation in a way that serves you, you will experience a fresh equilibrium. Still, going about your day with new awareness, you may at times feel the need for guidance. With a continuing better and deeper appreciation of your human life, and a mobilized will to live the best life possible, this is a good space in which to explore and master the guiding wisdoms.

CHAPTER FIVE

The Eleven Guiding Wisdoms

The Wisdom of Priorities
The Wisdom of Selectivity
The Wisdom of Simplicity
The Wisdom of Focus
The Wisdom of Attending to Intuition
The Wisdom of Seeking Permanent Happiness
The Wisdom of Asking Questions
The Wisdom of Reading
The Wisdom of Attending to Pain
The Wisdom of Doing Nothing
The Wisdom of God

The Wisdom of Priorities

In the second key to achieving equilibrium, "Prioritize Your Day," we looked at identifying your priorities for the remainder of your life. If you haven't identified your life priorities, if you are moved to—if you feel a sense of discovery and curiosity—on a clean sheet of paper write "My life priorities" and draw a circle around it. Ask your higher self how many you have. Perhaps it will be two, or three. The number is not important. What is important is knowing what is of fundamental importance to you this lifetime. As ideas and words come to your awareness, write them down, draw a line from the central circle and a circle around the newly written word or words. If you feel that you've got the area of priority but not its best expression, continue to cluster on an existing line or spoke from "My life priorities." Continue clustering with new ideas and clearer expressions of life priorities until you feel that the process is complete for now. Then go over what you've written. If you have more than the number of your life priorities, for each one ask your higher consciousness: *Is this my life priority?* For each one that is affirmed, put a checkmark in the circle.

Knowing your life priorities and acting with that wisdom can give you invaluable guidance. *It prioritizes your whole life.* This serves you as a foundation and guiding vision. Rather than going off on a tangent, a misadventure, if you can recall your life priorities and reconnect with their importance when faced with a questionable diversion or enticement, then you can more readily let go of it because you can know that it will not serve you. Giving attention and preference to your life priorities accords your life a cognizant direction and significance. There is no need to feel lost or disaffected, because you know what is important. Further, you can let go of things that would ordinarily rile you because, in your larger scheme of life, you know their relative unimportance. This is freeing.

When you are feeling freer, lighter, you may feel like dreaming about your life's possibilities. When it feels good, you may choose to sit comfortably indoors or outdoors and watch a slow, deepening sunset. You may feel like stretching, letting your hands reach high above you. You may choose to swim or run or walk. You may choose to cluster leisurely or with the quicksilver speed of inspiration that must be captured in words. However you are moved, you can use your intuitive nudges to dream about your life's possibilities. Perhaps whole new priorities will gather in your awareness. You may ask your higher self: *How can I make best use of my life?*

Getting in touch with the fact that you are a spiritual being having a human experience, a new priority may emerge. This may include aligning with who you want to become, what you wish to achieve, and how you want your life to count. This may be in your work or the love you bring to those with whom you share time, however short. This may also be how you wish to be further spiritualized—without even knowing what that means. Having faith—any faith— that you are being guided can instill confidence, independence, and felicity on your journey.

If this leads to your discovery of a new life priority or the refinement of an existing one, revise your list of life priorities. You may experience an awakened or energized purpose in moving through your life day by day. Living with a spiritual priority can readjust your life so that things matter, but not as much. You can detach from the whirl of news around you. Outcomes will come. They may not be what you hoped for, but because you are living with a spiritual priority, things looming in the future that previously you might have dreaded for the possible loss or crushing disappointment they could bring will not matter as much. With your increasing spiritual strength, you can keep things in better proportion. And with your wisdom of priorities, you realize that the proportions of things have themselves been reprioritized.

This is living afresh. This is living in a new now.

The Wisdom of Selectivity

Sometimes life can be so full and/or offer so many possibilities that it can feel like it is too much. This is where the wisdom of selectivity comes in. It's ever so easy to go through your day unconsciously immune to the idea that you have the inherent power and wisdom to select—and that you can muster the will to do so.

Even living with clear priorities, you are constantly being faced with choices. Often these are things your mind throws at you—things you want to do or have to do or would prefer not to do. Then there are the thoughts your mind presents—as if the thoughts were not a choice, but they are. Your mind constantly offers you an overflowing smorgasbord of things to think about, mull over, wonder about, revisit, worry about, and to project: what others think and feel, what might happen in an array of circumstances, and ongoing situations to entertain, as if those imagined futures and reimagined pasts were here and now.

Another major source of choices is other people. People present worlds of possibilities. There's who to text, email, call, and see. Then there's what to write or say and which emojis to insert. There's all that other people—many of whom are important and loved in your life—ask of you. There's what to do for whom. For holidays. For those who are ailing. And don't forget birthdays and anniversaries and the birthdays and cute pictures of pets to celebrate. Your response to all of this does not need to overrule what would better serve you. You have will and wisdom. Life can be an ongoing process of selection, wise selections that are aligned with your priorities and truly serve your best interests.

The internet and social media present endless choices that entice you. Throughout the day, many of us choose unconsciously or almost consciously where to visit and what to click, read, watch. We can spend so much time glued to our screens that we forget we're in a physical body.

You can give your body its due and wisely select from your physical smorgasbord. There are all the choices of what to eat and drink and what supplements to take. Unless you're blessed with a master genie who can materialize exactly what is best for you that you'll also thoroughly enjoy, you are faced with these selections. As you empower your higher self, you will find the desire and will to select what's best for you.

Further, don't forget that you are a sentient being with a physical body that thrives with movement. Rather than seeking a successful union with your recliner, get up. Learn to squat— that's one of the best stretches. (If it's too difficult, try squatting on a downward slope.) Also, review all the forms of physical activity and exercise you can engage in and select those that you would enjoy, would be best for you, and you would regularly engage in.

Becoming more aware of your many choices, you may wonder whether, rather than being at the passive effect of all these possibilities, there is any guidance that will empower you to select what you truly need, what's good, what's best. Can you select value and quality instead of being a passive consumer and reactor? Yes, here are three lenses or means for being aware of your choices and ascertaining what to select.

When faced with a choice, you can ascertain whether it feels like the next best thing for you, and whether it feels imperative, essential, and/or good. Feel the certainty of that knowing and then with that awareness you can act. Second, when you are choosing you can pause, enroll your sense of knowing, and ascertain to what degree you know it is necessary, beneficial, important, and/or a responsibility that is best fulfilled. If, while utilizing either of the lenses, you don't feel or see a clear answer, you can put that choice aside. That is freeing.

A third way is to ask God or your higher self: *What would Love select?* Here you are doing your best to align yourself with Love, to act wisely from that force of being. This may be the best guidance of all.

In developing the wisdom of selectivity, the issue or question is: To what do you want to give your attention and how do you want to expend your time (your life) wisely? In making selections, you may contend with lack of clarity, moral issues, money issues, quandaries of responsibilities, and the feelings of others and your own conflicting or muddled feelings. Knowing the factors at play, you can master the lenses you have to see clearly what is good, necessary, or true and select that.

The Wisdom of Simplicity

The mind complicates. The mind conjectures. The mind equivocates. The mind contextualizes. The mind considers. The mind questions. The mind issues a dictum, then a hankering, then a declaration, then a qualification, then an exception, and then gets lost in the issues they spawn.

We allow our minds to make things so complicated that we get confused. And then we can close to guidance. Some people thrive in complexity. Others, when faced with a soupçon of complexity, close down. To rise above the allurement of complexity or its overwhelm is to cultivate and choose simplicity. The enlightened practice of simplicity can guide you wisely.

For purposes of this exploration and discovery, simplicity used in these contexts means:

- The absence of counterproductive complexity in ideas, thoughts, and enterprises
- The freedom from excessive mental distractions and materialism
- The inherent clarity, purity, and/or beauty of ideas, communications, needs, and practices

Throughout, we are aiming for smart simplicity, knowing simplicity, vital simplicity that will facilitate the achievement of your daily goals and your continuing growth. We can achieve simplicity by utilizing the three *d*'s of simplicity: discrimination, detachment, and distillation.

Discrimination is discerning what is necessary or solely appropriate and letting go of the rest. A good example of where you can exercise discrimination to develop the wisdom of simplicity is entertainment. For many in our time, there are now four basic human needs: food, shelter, clothing, and entertainment. For some, our lives have become so full of entertainment that we are best defined by what shows we watch and games we play. This is what occupies our consciousness. This is the field in which we live. If you know that you are better balanced when you treat yourself to entertainment, ask yourself what is optimal for you to be engaged and balanced, while allowing time for whatever else is necessary or will enrich you. Perhaps you are best served when you devote two evenings a week to entertainment. Perhaps it is about an hour and a quarter five nights a week. Once you know your parameters (which naturally will shift as you go through life and practice your discrimination), discern what are the best entertainments for you and let go of the rest. If there's a series that friends are talking about, give it a try, and if it does not fully resonate with you, let go of it, and embrace a sleeker life in which you're not manifesting competing opinions and conflicting desires. That's growing in the wisdom of simplicity.

Detachment is being free—free of extraneous needs, expectations of others, and results. Being free of expectations of others means not being attached to what you imagine someone will say and how they will act. Perhaps you were really looking forward to seeing a particular movie with a friend. You arrive, buy your ticket, and then you receive a text that they aren't coming— they feel like staying home. Now, you might react with strong disappointment, with hurt and accusatory thoughts streaking through your mind throughout the movie. Or you could think, "This is for my greater good," let go of it, and enjoy the movie thoroughly. Perhaps the friend did show up and respected your mutual understanding of not talking during the film. The film enthralled you and you looked forward to sharing your enjoyment with your friend. Afterward, your friend opined that the film was a piece of junk and dismissed your enthusiastic comments. This could have greatly disturbed you, or if you simply let go of it, you would have been detached. Life is simpler without holding onto expectations.

Distillation is finding and knowing the essence of something and using or focusing on that to inform your awareness to the exclusion of potential distractions. A good example is desires. Let's say that you are beset by desires—burning desires that swirl around in your mind. They could be more time to pursue a creative calling, finding a great love, making more money, having friends with whom you can be yourself and share intimately, and/or healing a chronic health condition. The desires dart through your mind to the extent that you can feel dizzy figuring out how to satisfy them even when, for instance, you're needing to concentrate on something else.

When desires are occupying too much of your mental space, the object is to simplify your desires and distill them so that you are left with what is necessary, good, and promising. Thus, when you feel beset by desires and wish to feel freer and lighter, find a good time to review your desires. As you review your desires as to what's most pressing and also realistic to address at this time, with a detached attitude and focused intent, ask your higher self one or more questions about each desire that you select to resolve. For instance:

- Would it be in my highest and best good to let go of the desire to _____?
- Will fulfilling this desire allow me to feel complete?
- Does this desire need to be modified in any way? If yes, how?

- Is the desire to _____ best put on a back burner to entertain at a later time?
- Would it be in my highest and best good to attend presently
  to the desire to _____?
- If yes, what steps or actions might I take to allow me to realize the desire to _____?

You may wish to continue discovering how best to resolve
the desire as you see fit over any length of time. Feel free to take
notes and date them, make a voice recording or journal entry,
or whatever is best to externalize and specify these desires and
your clear intent about them in this moment. What you are doing
is distilling your desires, so that, first by focusing your attention
on a specific desire, you are heating it. Then, by being in touch
with your higher self and posing questions with a detached attitude, you are cooling your attachment to the desire so, ideally,
you are left with its purer, distilled state and the awareness of its
best place in your mental sphere and life, which have now been
simplified. You are also inculcating the wisdom to know what
is best for you.

The Wisdom of Focus

You can have worked on simplifying your life so that now it
is feeling streamlined, and at times you are feeling a welcome
lightness, clarity, and even joy. You may be attending to things
in your newly prioritized and simplified life. What if you keep
finding that things are not getting done? What if long after
you've engaged in a project or a task, you realize that you've

suffered a time skip? That is, the narrative of your life advanced without you being aware. You find that you've been in a different place, which you may not even recall, and you lost your focus. Have you ever been driving and sometime later realized you were driving and you had no idea what you had just been thinking about and how much time had elapsed? Having lost your focus, you were somewhere else entirely, and possibly endangered your life. The mind has a powerful habit of derailing you. Are you content to remain at its beck and call?

When you started the project (or whatever it was you were attending to), how strong was your focus? You can have definite intentions and the best day planned, but without focus, you will fail to be successful. Without focus, you lose out on life— at least the best life that you have discovered for yourself. It's more than attention. You can be attentive to the myriad things that cross your mind and, in the process, not accomplish want you want to.

The wisdom of focus is being attentive to where your attention is so that each time you realize you've left your focus, you return to that focus. It is also being determined to be focused each time you engage with something, be it driving, eating, a conversation, recreation, or being positive. In being positive, that means neutralizing negative thoughts and moods once they sweep over you and then returning to being positive again and again.

Clearly, for work, being focused is important. The mind can be a rogue elephant on a rampage or a crazed monkey on a bad mix of speed and cocaine. Your focus is your goad. That is, your focus guides your mental, physical, and emotional expression, bringing you back and back and back when you stray from your focus. Naturally, if you're engaged in work requiring intense concentration, you will profit from opportune breaks. And during your breaks, it is a good idea to focus on something pleasant, rather than the knotty problem you hoped to leave at your desk, in the yard, or wherever the problem is.

Don't expect to be super-focused overnight. It's a process. Simply being aware of your focus throughout the day is an important step. Focus is a guidance mechanism necessary to achieving what you want to achieve and being in the mental-emotional sphere you desire.

Take each moment at a time. Concentrate on one thing at a time. When your mind is straddling several things apparently simultaneously, you are scattered. Rather than multitasking efficiently, your attention is diluted, as is your access to your innate well of wisdom. Your well of wisdom is accessed in the eternal now.

Aspects of your mind can be run by fears and anxieties and all their permutations. For instance, concern may seem good, yet it's also a door to open and run through, charging into worry. If a concern announces itself, attend to it and ask if it needs to be dealt with now. If not, ascertain an appropriate time. When you do attend to it, determine whether you have the power to do anything about it; if so, what might you do; what steps are needed to accomplish your goal; and when would be a good time to focus on it. When that time comes, feel whether it is a good time to focus on it.

You gain much by having a main focus not only for specific tasks throughout the day, but also for each new day. You may advance your life by choosing a focus for different periods of weeks or months such as home improvements, getting in touch with valued friends with whom you're out of touch, introducing healthier food and new dishes into your diet, practicing the presence of God whenever you can remember, or planning a trip that you've been thinking about for years.

Focus facilitates the growth and fulfillment of your occupational, mental, emotional, physical, healthy, intimate, giving, and spiritual self. Adopting a particular focus and finding a way to fulfill it also serves to rebalance your life. Perhaps you have been giving and giving—to family in need, to organizations that need your services, to rescue dogs or cats. One evening you're tired, out of sorts, and you realize that you need to give yourself more intimate focus. From that realization, you may come up with a program to focus on your intimate needs for the next two weeks. That could include a massage, writing in your journal, seeing a romantic comedy, enjoying an intimate conversation with a kindred spirit, and setting aside times to envision what else you would love for your life that would feed you truly. This envisioning could introduce a whole new focus that you would welcome with a glad heart.

There's a certain satisfaction that you can enjoy from focusing on one thing and completing it. This can be a project at home or work, meditation, or being fully present with a partner or friend. When you are really focusing and returning to the focus when you realize your mind has strayed, there's a certain high that comes from concentration, to expanding into the eternal now. At such times, your intuition may more readily be accessed.

The Wisdom of Attending to Intuition

When a flash of intuition comes, you need to focus on it with keen awareness immediately. Otherwise it can dissipate without you receiving its insight. Intuition is immediate perception. It may be a distinct feeling or language that comes unbidden. The challenge is that when it comes unbidden, your active, thinking mind is typically busy-busy and you can miss it! That's why immediate focus is important.

Sometimes the intuition will be short and clear. You may want to write it down lest you forget it. Other times it may be something you need to pursue (emotionally, mentally, intuitively) and when you feel that you're there, focus on it, open it, unravel it. It may be a feeling that you need to sort through until you can articulate it.

Your intuition (that you know as well as you can to be true) can provide invaluable guiding wisdom. Living with the ongoing guidance of your intuition can elevate your life to a field of peace, ease, clarity, functionality, and achievement that you will cherish. Imagine intuition as a set of muscles you possess that you are able to develop. Those who go to a gym with a strong commitment to build beautiful bodies typically structure their days prioritizing the best times for their workouts, then focus intently on their workouts giving them their all, eat the best diets with the right timings and amounts of protein, take the optimal supplements, get enough sleep, lead simple lives, and may work out with the right trainer for them.

Likewise, your intuition is a faculty that you can develop to the level that you are operating in a better reality, a new now. It is mainly a commitment to work with yourself to be aware. In addition to delving into and knowing unbidden intuitions, you can learn to focus on *intuiting* truths about questions you have, guidance you seek. This can be as important as coming to know what is truly good in your life. If you are moved to, ask your higher self: *Dear higher self, what is truly good in my life?* You can let your higher self, your higher knowing, lead you to goodness after goodness, sensing whether each item is true.

If this feels too challenging, you can suss out what it is that you can know and affirm now. Start by naming areas of your life such as: relationships, creative expressions, desires, your journey this lifetime, and love. Sense what you are most pulled to ask about. If relationships, for instance, you can name those friends, relatives, business associations, animals—even God—that you are prompted to and ask: *To what extent is my relationship with _____ good?* Then explore the relationship, sussing out intuitively what is true and what might be enhanced or changed. For desires, you might have the desire to be better, to be kinder, and/or to be more positive. Thus, you might ask: *Dear nobler self, how might I be better?* Then explore the ways that arise in your consciousness. For your journey, you could ask: *How might I live to make best use of my life?* Perhaps one powerful way might be to live consciously in the present attuned to your higher sense of knowing. For love, you could ask: *Dear God, how can I better realize my potential for love?*

Intuitive guidance can help you in all kinds of situations. Perhaps you met someone special and you are unsure about the relationship. Two days later, you get a flash—call them—but then you think, "It's probably not a good time" or "Oh, it's too soon." Here's an example of when you need to break through your mental resistance and the dim reality of your thoughts and follow your intuition. Perhaps at the time you got the flash, the person was thinking of you, hoping you would call. Naturally, we don't have access to or control over the future, but the better and surer your intuition is, the more likely you will initiate all your actions at their optimal times and desist when you sense that is best.

You may dismiss intuition (your sense of knowing) as airy-fairy stuff, but give your higher self a chance to transform your life, opening to and receiving your inverted well of wisdom. Try a two-month experiment to practice attending to your intuition. Be open to and work with your higher self. Turn to God and ask to be more in tune with the Infinite. Then observe what comes through, what you discern, how you act, and the outcome.

If you begin to love more and more the idea of enhancing your intuition, even accessing it at will, there are ways to do this in which you can become proficient. Among the many methods are intuitive sussing, dowsing, and adept muscle testing. An important caveat is: each modality has any number of subtle requirements that, if not followed or met, may very well result in a false reading. Some of these subtle requirements may be aspects of your state of mind, hydration level, whether you are grounded, the wording of your questions, emotions and subjectivity that may block what is true or give false answers, and the way you perform the modality or technique. It is best to learn from a master or someone who is nearly a master. Then once you feel you have reached a level of proficiency—it could well be after years of intense focus—your higher consciousness may lead you to a better, personalized way of intuiting.

Don't we just want to know? With growing proficiency, you can ask yes or no questions, questions that are best gauged by degree or percentages, and even if you feel that you need to ask or know something but don't know what it is, you can ask which questions to ask. Something to be aware of is that when you get answers, your sense of knowing can nudge you as to whether what you are getting is true or not. If not, then something needs to be changed—the wording or ordering of your asking, your mental or physical condition, or distortion by a negative influence that needs to be cleared.

What is the wisdom of attending to intuition? Simply, it is to lead the best life possible, being informed, flowing knowingly through each day. Further, as you exercise your sense of better knowing, your consciousness is evolving and transforming into a higher and deeper state of contentment and happiness.

The Wisdom of Seeking Permanent Happiness

Now that you've been developing your intuition, why not entertain the possibility of something audacious: *You can seek and ultimately attain permanent happiness*. This can be inspiriting and life-changing.

This harks back to knowing yourself and learning what brings happiness. It harks back further to knowing who you truly are—a being of unalloyed bliss, love, and joy. Before you ever came to this world, your existence was beyond language.

Joy, love, sheer happiness—call it whatever limiting word you choose. If your existence was this state of indescribable happiness, it can once again become that unadulterated happiness and be that wonder, on and on and on, *beyond time.*

First, there's the invitation to entertain and accept the possibility. Second, there's the call to research the real road to happiness and discover sages through the ages and what promise they hold for you. Then there is the challenge of faith—having faith that it can be attained—regardless of the dead ends and disappointments you encounter in your search and experience.

The duping, settling, and downfall of many is that they believe they can find happiness in that which is temporary—by acquiring material possessions or people or fame or power. But these all leave you at some point. The less we identify with the outer, the fleeting, the less we are attached to and the more space we have for the in-filling of our happiness. Eventually, we must give back everything. Before we dematerialize in fire or earth, our hands hold nothing. Gone are the people that moved our hearts. Gone are the rooms that made us feel special. This may sound like a harsh critique, but it is freeing.

What is critical to distinguish is what can give you temporary happiness and what can allow you to become permanent happiness. This is strategic. This is smart. This is a way to satisfy the chronic panging wants of your mind but also the oft-suppressed yearning of your soul, which gets mistakenly translated into the wants of your mind.

It is important to know your mind and work with it, for that will keep you balanced and treading your searching path. Satisfying your daily changing needs and desires—knowing they can at best bring temporary happiness—while also seeking your path to permanent happiness is smart and strategic because it is sustainable. This sustains you because it brings a measure of contentment, satisfying your needs to keep you balanced, without losing your focus.

If you adopt this focus—seeking permanent happiness—it will reorder your life and inspire you to till the wisdom of attending to your intuition and asking questions. Each of us has our own unique path. While it may give you a sense of security, copycatting the steps and diversions on the path of others can be misleading, taking you further away from your path. Your vain reward then was false hope and possibly a dangerous diversion.

It is best to simply start where you are. You can find the first golden bricks of your yellow brick road. You are there. First, ask your higher self: *Do you want to seek permanent happiness?* If not, skip to the next section. Or if you are moved to, read on here, as this may give you valuable guidance.

If in your heart of hearts, you wish to realize permanent happiness, understand that you will need to leave the physical world (for good), then your mind (your thinking self), to exist purely as soul, realizing ever more divine states ultimately to merge back into the Source of being, the Godhead. If you want to realize permanent happiness but do not believe in reincarnation or existence after death, that is okay. You can seek it anyway. You may benefit from the guiding process in the next section, "The Wisdom of Asking Questions."

If you decide to seek permanent happiness, you may be undertaking a journey now that you had not imagined was possible and waiting for you. With your best awareness, you just need to take the next step. Then another. When you are not sure of "what next," check in with yourself and sense your higher knowing. Perhaps reviewing "The Wisdom of Doing Nothing" or "The Wisdom of Reading" will trigger an idea, an inspiration, a way. The journey to complete happiness is an extraordinary one that few are blessed to take. Along the way, unexpected "happenstances" may lead to seeming miracles or setbacks. Accept it all. Through it all, exercise your willingness and ability to ask questions, as the responses you receive will keep you going toward your lodestar, your cherished goal of happiness.

The Wisdom of Asking Questions

Embrace the idea that your life is a treasure hunt. You may actually have treasures waiting for you to recover them. At this point, you probably don't know *what kinds* of treasure are in store for you. You may have inklings, but you don't know. You are on a journey, walking over rolling green hills with lush valleys, tough chaparral, and unexpected encounters. Beyond the hills is the future. You can't see it because the hill in front of you is blocking your view. Even when you get to the top, what is waiting for you may be hidden in dense foliage or under a bed of ivy. And beyond: valleys and hills, and valleys and hills that you can't yet see. The point is: keep going.

Love the idea that your life still has treasures that are meant for you. Your growing awareness will help you figure out where to go and look. What may give you invaluable help is asking questions. In life, we're not provided with treasure maps or navigation systems with authoritative voices that correct our every wrong turn. That is why, in endeavoring to live the best life possible for you, it is essential to ask questions. Asking the right questions can transport you to a new field of possibilities.

It is easy to go through life like a stimulus-response automaton. You hear something, you see something, you think something—you react. *You give away that part of your life to what you have allowed to capture your attention, will, and time.* (Examples among myriads are: the phone rings: you answer it; you see a link: you click or tap it, then another; you think something, then something else, then forty minutes later, you realize you've forgotten what you had decided to do.) When you take the next step, how often do you question whether this is where and how you truly want to be spending your life? Competing forces want your attention, your time, your body, and your money. Your life.

When do you ever look for the underlying assumptions in how you live your life and the decisions you make and then ask: *Is this good? Is this best for me? What would be optimal?*

One of the wisdoms of asking questions is that you are exercising your wisdom of selectivity. In so doing, you strengthen your wisdom of intuition and your wisdom of being true to yourself. Asking questions can ultimately lead you to the treasures awaiting you. Asking questions can also help lead you through each day, so that by the end of the day, you feel content because you have done your best to live the best day possible.

An orientation of asking questions puts you in a different frame of mind. Rather than being at the effect of all those competing forces, as you walk through the tall, thick grasses, you are picking your way, choosing your paths, avoiding the brambles (and any snakes that may be lying in wait), giving yourself well-deserved rests, pausing to breathe in the good air, giving thanks, and if a ladybug alights on your arm, making an innocent wish before she flies away.

Remember when you were a child? Always asking questions. Those who ask, consider the answers, and when their curiosity prompts them to ask even more searching questions, seem to come into themselves more fully and get on better in the world. Further, by questioning assumptions, you can wake up to the truth, overturn conventional thought, and/or discover a whole new path. Asking questions enlivens you. You are seeking to know and live in truth and improve your life.

When asking questions, it is important to be emotionally detached so that the answers can be as accurate as possible. Because your brain and body are mainly comprised of water, it is also important to be sufficiently hydrated when doing intuitive and energy work. You may find it helpful or enlightening to ask any of the following:

> Am I thinking too much about _____? If yes, what would be the best way to resolve it?
> Who are the best people for me to spend time with? (This can also be modified to address a specific issue with someone.)
> What creative expression might I best engage in?
> When considering whether to do something, ask: is it in my highest and best good, safe and appropriate to _____?
> What is the next best thing for me to do?
> What experiences would help me feel complete in my journey this lifetime?

> ➢ Do I have a higher source of truth? If so, what might I call it now?
> ➢ How can I live as my aware self?
> ➢ What is my purpose for being here, this lifetime?

It is also important to begin your questions by addressing what you consider a higher source of truth. Thus, you can begin questions by asking within: *Dear higher self,* or *Dear higher consciousness,* or *Dear God,* or whatever brings you in better tune with the source of truth. As you continue to evolve on your journey, you may find that asking the following questions to be of transcendent value, especially if you are seeking permanent happiness.

> ➢ When faced with a decision, ask higher consciousness or God: *Dear God, will _____ take me closer to true happiness?*
> ➢ When pondering something, ask God: *Dear God, is _____ true?*
> ➢ When wanting guidance, ask God: *Dear God, what are the best questions to ask?*

You may receive the answer once you ask, or seven hours later, or three days later when you least expect it. If you feel doubt about what comes through, it may be best to let go of the question, as the time to know may not yet have arrived. It is always best to distinguish between your thinking thoughts and the experience of surety of what resonates as true. With your growing sense of knowing, when you know or feel the answer, you can muster the confidence to proceed.

Curiosity about truth, God, your spiritual and/or worldly

purpose for being here, and also longing for self-realization will fuel your evolution. In addition to asking questions and attending to your intuition, you may feel the need for a knowing companion that can offer engaging issues to ponder and vicarious experiences to enrich you.

The Wisdom of Reading

We can gain much by reading. Many of those who have gone before us and delved into the mysteries of how to live have left their distilled wisdom for us in books. They were lost at various times in their lives, and they found a way through the brambles and thorns, over the hill, to a new place of vantage, and later recorded their experiences. If they did not record them, someone they inspired did so.

Reading (or listening) to the right book at the right time is a blessing. Reading can deliver new worlds to you as you relax in a favorite chair, let go on your couch or bed, or escape from a jet flight to a world of your choosing. Spiritual books, personal growth books, memoirs, or novels can transform you by affording you the luxury of vicarious experience that you can try on, go through, learn from, as it enriches you. As you delve deeper into the art of living, good books can be the best companions, giving you guidance, lessons learned, pitfalls suffered, and recoveries made.

A good book can become a great book when you actively read the book, allowing it to expand your field of experience, but also questioning and testing it against your own sense of knowing. Claims, statements, pronouncements—do they have the ring of truth? If you doubt some claim, usher in your sense of knowing. Is it true? If you simply don't know, if either side could be true, accept the doubt and that this is something you don't know *presently*. Thus, you can test your wisdom and enrich it but also engender humility and a sense of where you would like your wisdom to expand.

In addition to improving your understanding of everything under the sun but also that which is beyond the sun, the worlds you take in can increase your empathy and enhance your sense of self. You are not the only one struggling. You can learn from those who have gone before. The most interesting people are those who read—not those who want to impress others with their reading or those who only want to lose themselves to escape from their own reality. The people who actively engage with their reading are also those who enliven themselves with that interaction.

You can practice your intuition to find the right book at the right time. You have a sense of where you are on your journey and thus can utilize that sense of knowing to find and join with a felicitous companion. If you are curious about a question, a metaphysical philosophy, a meditation practice, or how to thrive in love with a certain kind of person, the well-chosen book can enlighten you and save you from wasted excursions into unhelpful experience. Books are also catalysts for further exploration, pointing you to "what next."

Especially when you feel that your life is tough, dreary, or lacking, the right-chosen book can be a wonderful comfort. If a story is fine and true, you can live along with the characters, going deeper into their lives, vicariously experiencing their struggles, seeing them fall and rise and, ultimately, what makes them better humans. Stories and fables also afford you the luxury of trying on alternate lives without having to suffer deprivations or pay the price for causing pain. In so doing, you can learn how other people live and hopefully develop more empathy. A finely evolved person automatically feels and expresses empathy. Empathy separates the wise from the self-absorbed. A person devoid of empathy cannot begin to appreciate the pain of another. Yes, books are also a comfort because they mitigate the pain of life, the pain of people. You can see how others have overcome tremendous challenges and suffering to pass through the fires of life, chastened and wiser.

The Wisdom of Attending to Pain

Pain is a message, a warning system. Something is out of balance. Possibly, that something is struggling to return to equilibrium.

When you become conscious of a pain, your first impulse may be to ignore it, to continue pursuing whatever current desire is ordering your attention. When the pain returns, you may act on an even stronger impulse to ignore it, to open a drawer of your mind, hide the pain, close the drawer, and forget about it. There are pains that will resolve themselves on their own, either through the majesty of your master inner healer or simply life— experiences washing through your consciousness, sweeping out that particular trouble.

The flip side of failing to attend to pain is over-attending to it to the point that all your worried focus makes it worse. The wisdom you seek is when and how to attend to pain. This can

change by the day, hour, and minute. It depends on the conflu-
ence of many factors. The four main types of pain are physical, mental, emotional, and existential. A pain may comprise as
many as all four. The more chronic and involved the pain, the
more likely it is that it involves more than the physical manifes-
tation. While life may be likened to the ebb and flow of pleasure
and pain—the riot of duality—pain attended to well may help
you achieve a higher, more informed state of equilibrium, and
also further your evolution.

If after ignoring a pain, it returns and returns again, and even
morphs into a different kind of pain, the pain may represent a
journey you are being offered. That journey may be for a day,
a fortnight, or the rest of your life. Unless your inner healer
resolves the pain, either by ignoring the pain or answering the
call to attend to the pain, your life is going to change. Either way,
you may find yourself getting sicker and sicker, and even meeting your death. But by answering the call, you can ask for the
grace to receive the gift of accessible intuition. Depending on
where you turn, whose care you seek, utilizing your intuition
keenly may make all the difference.

Legion are the stories of wrong diagnoses, surgeries with
unattended consequences, toxic pill regimens, ongoing ther-
apeutic relationships that get you nowhere except a reduced
bank balance. The message here is: don't give away your will,
ignoring your inherent power to know what is best for you now.
Just because someone has certain credentials or impresses you
with their professional status doesn't mean that they are your
best bet—that they will eradicate the pain and resolve your
condition.

Each person you go to for help may sincerely try to do their best, but they only bring their training, experience, and judgments, which may be biased, faulty, and misdirected. You can always say no. You can always pray humbly for guidance. If you are plagued with doubt, you don't have to act. You can take a step back, rest, and, when the time is right, renew your research to gather information. Healing goes hand in hand with taking responsibility for your well-being. This harks back to: don't give away your will and your power. Your distressed body, psyche, and person is not a car that you can drop off at a dealer for a 30,000-mile service. Beware of conventional "wisdom," unnecessary procedures, and depressing prognoses that very well may be the limitations of a professional that are paraded before you as the answer—the final word on your troubles—to make you step in line and follow orders.

Regard and embrace your intuition as your lifeline—for better life and even for further life. Certain of our physical diseases originated in mental and/or emotional stress and the challenge is to find the right process (and often processes) to peel away the layers, find and pierce the hurt, allow the poisons to escape, fill your psyche with revitalizing energy, and allow the wound to heal. Depending on the hurt, it is a process that may take much dedication, sessions, and time to pursue.

But the wisdom of attending to pain is that you are being guided to a better life, a life that is more healed, whole, and energized to advance you to a higher state of being and love.

Regard major pains and their concomitant conditions as projects. This can introduce detachment and clearheadedness that will help keep negative emotions in check and also help

you make the right decisions. Be wary—we can become so dedicated to our projects that they define who we are. You may feel
so minimized or overwhelmed that your pain projects become
your stories. When you meet people, you tell them your pain
story, unaware of what is best for them and you. In this telling
of your pain and procedures, you ignore the ongoing sparking
love within you while you talk on mindlessly, even oblivious as
well of the love people may be giving you.

Don't allow your project to take over your life. Attend to each
pain project when you feel sufficiently mobilized and the time
is right. If you keep putting off things you feel you should do,
question why (and release guilt if it arises). If you still haven't
contacted that professional, is it perhaps that you don't actually
need to see them now, or is it perhaps some barrier you need to
surmount? Maybe you need to allow time just for you—a mini
vacation from your pain projects where you can let go and your
spirit can be replenished. Be it watching a fun show, enjoying a
delicious meal, immersing yourself in glorious music, or taking
a short trip to be in the beauty of nature, you can wisely choose
your vacation away from your over-attending to pain.

Some maintain that stress is the root of all disease. The
stresses may have arisen from abuse when you were a child and
self-sabotaging subconscious beliefs formed as the result of the
abuse. Making your way in the world as a child and teenager
may have added all kinds of stress along with your still-bur-
ied, unhealed hurts. Then stresses build throughout life: the
stress of doing and trying so much—attending to family, jobs,
home, shopping for food and clothes, getting meals together,
exercising, and with the pain projects heaped on, that creates

even more stress. And this is on top of the original stressors and traumas that created the self-defeating subconscious beliefs, programming, and armoring that may be keeping good health from returning to you.

Gifted healers can help you unravel self-sabotaging subconscious beliefs and facilitate their release and, with you, rescript and reprogram these and bring about whole brain rebalancing with health-affirming beliefs. Further, there are healers who, working with different modalities, can allow you to return to your point of homeostasis, the place of equanimity and zero stress in which your master inner healer can be activated and empowered to work on and heal one high priority after another.

It is wonderful to pursue feeling good, to resolve the pain and to transform yourself into being as well as you can be. Still, a certain pain may nag you. Either when you are lost in your aloneness or in a crowded room of people. You have been attending to your healing. You may be feeling better than you have in a long time. Even so, something nags.

It may be a feeling of something missing, an indefinable longing, of not feeling at home, or that love is incomplete—that you want to be filled and overflow with love, that nothing else will ever fully satisfy you. Just being here, we bear the assaults of life. Have you ever wondered, have you really wanted to know: *Why am I here? Do I have a purpose? Has anyone solved the mysteries of existence?* These intimations and questions may be expressions of existential pain.

This is the pain that has been expressed in humankind's immortal questions: Why am I here? Is God real? Is there life after death? Do I have a purpose this lifetime? Why do bad things happen to good people? Is there meaning in the world?

If you are aware of any of these questions, if you ask them and ponder them, then you are taking steps toward attending to your existential pain. Being aware that you exist and feeling moved to know the answers to your questions is wise. This is a divine guidance system. We are born with the sense of discrimination so that we may be guided to grow in wisdom. Your existential pain is your opportunity to embark on or continue your journey of realization. The more self-realized you become, the more profoundly your stress of existential pain is resolved.

To be aware of your existential pain and discover "what next" on your journey, you could explore this by doing nothing.

The Wisdom of Doing Nothing

Doing nothing is a gift you give yourself. Once a day, let go of the urge to do. Set aside three minutes or twelve minutes or whatever time works for you, sit comfortably in a favorite room or outside, and just look and let your thoughts slip away, like a tree's autumn leaves falling to the ground. Let your vision alight on objects, noticing the light on a piece of furniture, a lamp, the masses of bright light or soft, green sheen on leaves. Notice the differences in colors the light makes. Let yourself enjoy the highest good in simply being.

Give yourself the gift of not having to think about things. You can let your awareness take in what you are observing, not paying heed to any thoughts that drift into your mind. Or you can do repetition of an affirmation or a name of God. Regard repetition as emptying and cleansing the vessel. Whenever you are aware that you're thinking, simply return to what you are repeating. Doing repetition supersedes your streaming thoughts and can elevate your consciousness.

What dreams may come when you let yourself be?

Inspirations may come to you. Knotty problems may unknot unbidden, and now your course is clear.

At times we think we need to do something, when, if we paused and felt how we feel, we'd realize that we don't feel like it. The situation may be that we really don't need to—there won't be negative consequences if we don't do it. This is when it is good to clear your mind and access what feels good.

When you are doing nothing, you are going deeper into the eternal now. You are creating the space for the presence of God, and that may become known to you. You are being your humble self, clearing your mind as best you can.

If you think of yourself as a cup or chalice, doing nothing, just being with your being, is emptying your cup. Sitting without expectations, giving thanks for your awareness of your being is righting your cup. Being positive fills your cup—with positive purpose, with a sense of direction, and yes, with grace.

Sitting, doing nothing is something you might come to love and return to daily. Not being lost in doing, you are nudging yourself into a truer reality. You are opening your being so that you can receive wisdom. This is the wisdom that is beyond language. It is immersing yourself in a higher state of being. It may be only for some moments, but in those timeless moments, you are released from the shackles of time and, thus freed, your being expands toward God, the ultimate source of wisdom.

The Wisdom of God

Can you entertain a heterodoxy? Perhaps several? A heterodoxy is a statement, belief, or view not in accord with established or accepted doctrines or opinions, especially in theology. If you believe in, can provisionally accept, or entertain the existence of a Supreme Being that is omniscient, omnipresent, and all-loving, you are faced with a conundrum. The conundrum is that divine Spirit is not readily discernible with your physical senses and intellect. You (and others) may have had apparent tastes of the divine—for instance, experiences of pure exaltation, inner swellings of grace—that transcend language. But identifying and verifying the existence of that Supreme Spirit remains elusive.

If the confirmation of that very existence is (for now) beyond you, how do you receive the guiding wisdom of God? And how do you know that is what it is?

First, don't buy into the idea that any belief in the existence of God is a self-gratifying, deceptive, delusional indulgence. Don't believe that God is dead, or far from you, or does not care about you. Do not entertain or embrace the notion that God has cast you away because of your egregious actions.

The trick and challenge of living on the physical plane is discriminating that the everlasting and thus truly real is invisible, while that which we accept as real changes, disappears, and is not real. Our bodies and the things around us are grand illusions of almost entirely empty space—atoms masquerading as solid stuff. If you are willing to and can entertain the notion of a unifying force of omniscience and an infinite field of being, that

Being of Love *is here now for you*. That Supreme Being is closer than your heartbeat, yet the complete evolution to knowing is a seemingly endless journey. But along the way, precious clues of guidance can be known. You can choose to tune in, while you tune out the noise of your mind and the strictures of time, and open a space of possibility and faith.

In other words, you can be your best self, being as virtuous and spiritually strong as you can (along with the missteps). By being that way and tuned in to the power within, you can turn to that unifying field for guidance. This is a heterodoxy. That Perfect Love is perfectly willing for you to turn within for guiding wisdom. The challenge is discriminating between your mind and that highest guidance. If we're not following our indiscriminate impulses or the minds of others, we are typically following the dictates of our minds, which are generating the same programs again and again. (Why do some people, in effect, marry the same person three times?) How can this give us true, guiding wisdom?

Because we are ruled to a large extent by the passions that feed and generate more ego, anger, greed, attachment, and lust, we are up against an awful lot when we strive to be our nobler self. For now, one key is to tune in to and listen to your conscience. Until you have attained an element of elevation to a surer field of wisdom, let your conscience be your guide. Step by step, stage by stage, your conscience can evolve into your omniscience. The archaic meaning of conscience is inmost thought or sense, knowledge of inner self. Your inmost self, your soul, is part and parcel of God.

Yes, the conundrum is that God is beyond the mind, which is our default operating system. For the most part, mind is what we live in and live for. Yet, right here now, LoveSource knows best. We are living a play whose script we don't know, yet we speak our lines with polished ease.

A key to sanity, to spiritual sustenance is humility. A first step is imbibing humility and accepting that we don't necessarily know what is best for us. We don't know how and why we will be tested, purified, refined, spiritualized, prepared, made ready for a higher reality, a new now. For now, embrace the audacious, soaring vision that this lifetime you can come into and be increasingly guided by the wisdom of God. This is a heterodoxy you can come to love. God has no limitations—people mistakenly attribute limitations to that Supreme Power.

Have patience, faith, a true heart. If you let yourself accept or have faith in an omnipresent omniscience, you are opening yourself to receive guidance. Here are three ways you can do your best to receive and be guided by the wisdom of God.

First, focus on your higher self. Develop your intuition, your sense of higher knowing. Bat away negativities and mind-insistent judgments.

Second, develop and listen to your conscience, your moral compass. Regard your conscience as your true north. If you face a dilemma, which way does your true moral compass point? What would God do?

Third, imagine that God has taken human form and is with you always. This is the best friend you could ever hope for, with no self-interest and only wanting your good welfare. When you don't know or aren't sure, turn to your all-loving friend and guide and ask. With your true friend, to whom you can always turn, you need not have a worry in the world.

CHAPTER SIX

The Ten Keys to Achieving Equilibrium

The Second Five Keys

Resolve Your Worries
Balance Being, Doing, and Having
Find Freeing Fun
Allow Things to Arrive in Their Own Time
Schedule Winsome Relaxation

Resolve Your Worries

Worries can keep popping up, running through your thoughts, seizing your awareness. It's as if a rodent bot is running along the coils of your brain pricking you with its sharp nails. When you are worrying, your attention is divided and negative. Worrying prevents you from moving forward with an aligned purpose, confidence, and lightness. Worrying prevents you from being in the now.

Worry undermines your life and cherished goals. It is evidence that you lack faith in yourself to rise to each occasion with grace, assurance, and the best competence you can muster for each occasion. If you believe in God, worry shows that you lack faith in God and what you can accomplish with that grace and guidance. Even those who are spiritually evolved can worry a lot. The negative, lower mind is a powerful usurper of carefree, happy awareness. If you have well-worn worry grooves, this is indeed a challenging habit to overcome. It's important to do so if you want to achieve and enjoy equilibrium.

Regardless if you worry like a voracious shrew driving off well-intentioned rival thoughts or worry like a sparrow pecking at pebbles, you possess practical tools to resolve your worries. A good way to begin to resolve your worries is to list them in one of three classifications: whether it's a) something you can do something about, b) something that can best be handled with the assistance of another, or c) something over which you have no power. No matter how seemingly minor, list your worries in a note-taking app, a word processing program, a journal, or on pages of blank paper.

Once you create the three groups, observe your thoughts throughout the day, and each time you notice that you are worrying, name the worry and enter it in one of the three classifications or groups. When the same worry comes through again, place a checkmark or another mark next to its entry. It will be revealing to know you entertained a particular worry five times, ten times, or more during the day.

To assist you in identifying your worries, the three prime worries involve money, body, and people. These worries are projected onto the future, present, and past. Money worries include how will I pay for medical bills, credit card balances, loans, education, an emergency, housing costs (increasing, known, and unforeseen), and my older years? Whether the bills are already due or will come due, or you are worrying about an investment, money worries are the prime worry for most people.

The second major worry involves your body, with worries and mental chatter revolving like: am I fat, am I attractive, will I get cancer, what will happen to me as I grow old, what do other people think about my appearance, am I eating too much / too little gluten, greens, soy, dairy, fat, or processed foods, and what can I change to make me look better? If we're brave enough to take a good look in the mirror without clothing, we might ask: what can I do about my love handles, muffin top, thinning hair, beer belly, too small (or sagging) breasts, wrinkles, hairiness (or lack of hair), bad skin, sagging behind, poor posture, lack of muscles, man boobs, and / or varicose veins?

The third major worry involves people: what can I / should I do about this relationship, does so-and-so still love me / like me, will I find someone to love, what are those people doing to our country, who can I find for sex, will my client like my work, what is so-and-so saying about me, and what does he / she think about me?

To resolve a worry, first identify whether the worry is an actual problem. If it is not, realize that your mind is obsessing—it's stuck in this worry groove. It needs to have the program erased or overwritten. Here are three ways to do that. The first is "Will over Worry." As soon as a worry pops into your awareness, emphatically think *Cancel*, then breathe easily, and acknowledge lightly: *The lower mind is just doing its thing.* If you have a free moment or longer, occupy your mind with something positive. That can be doing repetition, playing with a pet, reading a good book, or watching a funny or uplifting video.

If a worry (that's not a problem) keeps cropping up, you can disentangle it and get to the root of it. This second process of resolving your worries is called "Uproot and Harvest Your Worry." For instance, perhaps you have acknowledged that you want to take a trip, but you are worrying whether you can physically pull it off and/or pull yourself together to do all the preparation. You're worrying about how to get there, where to stay, what to pack, and/or what to do once you get there. Perhaps you feel overwhelmed. This is not a problem. It's simply a matter of taking a regular disciplined approach. First list in descending order what elements of the trip you are most anxious about. If you are going to be terribly busy before the trip but have already committed to the trip mentally and/or financially, estimate the time it will take to complete your research, reservations, activity planning, and other preparations. This process will also enable you to ascertain whether you will have sufficient time to complete your preparation.

If after listing your concerns and beginning to look into how much more research, planning, and contacting you need to do, you may feel that the trip is too much—beyond your planning capabilities, too expensive, too much work (considering your other commitments), or too stressful before, during, and/or after the trip. Modifying or canceling the trip for those dates is an option. What would best help you return to equilibrium? Even if canceling means losing money after you've obtained whatever refunds you can, you need to weigh the loss of funds versus the stress.

If after delving into your concerns, you are feeling more positive about the trip, then you need to plot what you need to plan and resolve from now until you depart. To help you feel less anxious and stressed about the trip, perhaps this worry is best resolved by spending forty-five minutes after dinner each evening looking at places to stay and things to do there in order to move toward completing your arrangements.

The third process is called "Releasing Patterns Releases Worries." For instance, do you worry about having enough time? Do you rush and stress to get to an appointment on time? Alternatively, are you habitually late? Does either adversely affect your health, relationships, commitments, and positive sense of self? If either pattern is true, you might think of this as a problem, but it is more an issue of your mental wiring and deeply rooted issues. If you find yourself repeating self-defeating patterns, you may need to seek a professional to assist you in identifying and releasing the conscious and subconscious beliefs that are running you and not serving you. Unless you can do the work yourself, doing the research and using your intuition could assist you well in finding the right person. This good work can take time and financial commitment, but doing it could be liberating, delivering you to a better day-to-day reality, an easier new now.

If the worry is an actual problem, you can take positive steps to resolve it regardless of whether the worry is in either of the three groups or classifications. Perhaps you worry about having enough money. Is this for the rest of the month, or the rest of your life? If the money worry is for the rest of the month, you can start by preparing a budget. If you feel this is beyond your ability, you can seek assistance from a professional or a personal contact for whom, ideally, you can do something in return. Not having enough money may be able to be resolved by reducing expenses, increasing income, or both. Or by negotiation—if you have received a bill that you feel is outrageous, you can ask for clarification from the billing party and/or seek information on comparable billing practices. If after having done sufficient research, you still feel that it is outrageous, you now are armed with some tools for negotiation. When money is a problem, the key is: don't be passive, thinking everything will sort itself out, or eventually you'll win a lottery. Unless, your intuition is clearly guiding you to do nothing, you are falling deeper into debt and anxiety.

Health concerns are other common worries. If this is a chronic worry, you might have health anxiety, which is when almost anything can set off a worry that you are sick and have or are developing a severe illness. Even if you have had tests, especially repeated tests, you could be suffering from health anxiety. If so, it can be treated by the right professional.

If you feel that your health concerns are definite or may be the sign of something, then it is important for you to *take responsibility* to resolve what is going on. Revisit the section, "The Wisdom of Attending to Pain" in Chapter Five. You may be able to resolve the health concern on your own, or you may need the assistance of another. One key is don't allow your will to be subjugated or your intuition to be suppressed. You can always get a second opinion, especially if you are feeling doubts about a procedure that is ordered or recommended. You can decline or stop treatments, or find new, hopeful ones. When you take responsibility, especially for a chronic health concern, you may be facing a project that lasts a long time. The point is to be "all in" and, in so doing, do your best to have a relaxed mind, feel good about being proactive, and resolve worries if they arise.

Worry about potential disasters can become real problems. If you worry about hurricanes, for instance, a big one wreaking havoc, you can do your best to dispel this worry, although you have no power over them. You can do research as to what extent hurricanes will grow in the period you expect to live where you do. You can make a decision as to whether to stay or leave. If you decide to stay, you can have hurricane-safe windows installed, disaster supplies kits and other preparation in place, clear evacuation plans, and contact phone numbers. Also, ensure that you have adequate insurance. If, in spite of your good efforts at preparation, you continue to worry, you can seek professional help to allay this anxiety.

Resolving your worries allows you to be more fully in the now. The mind is obstinate and loves repetition and well-worn grooves, especially worry grooves. Releasing your worry patterns is an ongoing process that can be pursued with detachment. The more you are worry-free, the better you are empowered to be in the eternal now and pursue your best life, open to your higher guidance.

Balance Being, Doing, and Having

The three modes of our conscious lives are being, doing, and having. A vital key to achieving equilibrium is to bring them into balance each day as well as you can. What might be interesting and beneficial would be for you to draw a pie chart, showing on average what percent of your conscious day is devoted to being, doing, and having. First, review days you have lived recently and months ago. You may want to jot down for each group examples of things you did, like watching TV, daydreaming about buying a new car, working, eating, and sitting outside, looking at nature. Also enter the estimated times devoted to each.

Having is focused on acquisition, consumption, and control. Examples of having are: desiring to have something or someone for whatever purpose, thinking about buying something, enjoying your possessions, maintaining your dwelling and yard the way you want them, being in a room looking at your favorite stuff, and admiring your body or another's.

Being is focused on awareness of existence, personal and spiritual connection, love, and advancement toward self-realization. Examples of being are: sitting outside doing nothing, being grateful, praying, meditating, feeling your feelings, being aware of what passes between you and another, and being loving. Simply having fun, when you're detached from winning or making points, would be a state of being.

Doing is focused on being active, getting things done, accomplishing. Satisfaction, relief, and/or security can be derived from the process of doing and completing. Examples of doing are:

checking your phone, driving, losing yourself in social media, app/web browsing, working while you eat and text, playing games, and searching for something to watch and watching.

Once you have a feeling about how your conscious time breaks down, intuit and estimate on average what percent of your recent waking life has been devoted to doing, having, and being. A pie chart is simply a circle divided by lines radiating from the center that make the sections look like pieces of pie. Typically, your pie chart might show doing as the biggest piece of pie at 61%, having at 24%, and being at 15%. Someone whose main pleasure is the material world might have a pie chart that shows doing at 50%, having at a hefty 44%, and being at a little bitty 6%. For someone who meditates and contemplates a lot, their pie chart might show doing at 63%, having at 5%, and being at 32%.

Simply intuit which numbers represent what average portions of your waking life are doing, having, and being, and then draw your pie chart. Now, contemplate what you found. How alive, how vivacious are you during different phases of your doing, having, and being? For you, in this period of your life, how balanced are your doing, having, and being? How well is the time and attention devoted to each mode serving you?

We are called human beings, however most of us devote a fraction of our waking time to being. Joy comes in higher states of being and also when losing yourself while you are giving yourself to a higher, nobler cause. What can you do to balance being, doing, and having?

Ask yourself: *In my life, what would love add, reduce, enhance, enjoy, let go, set aside time for, and imbibe with gratitude and love?*

Scan your life, noting what you do throughout the day and also infrequently (for example, once a month, several times a year) and see what love would add, reduce, enhance, enjoy, let go, set aside time for, and/or imbibe with gratitude and love. Perhaps what might come up is adding good moments before you eat to gaze at your food with gratitude. Perhaps you will let go of looking at social media before bed or while you'd like to be working. Take notes and integrate these changes into your life.

What is important is not only the relative time devoted to each of the modes of existence, but also the *quality* and *positivity* and *aliveness* of each particular expression of doing, having, and being. Even while listening to someone and feeling bored, forgetting something, chewing your food, being awake when you want to be asleep, and waking up remembering what you're meant to do today, it is transformative to be aware of each moment of these seemingly different expressions and experiences of existence while doing your best to summon an atmosphere of love. With your new dynamic balance, life should feel more like you want it to feel, more like you are feeding yourself in all the areas and ways you need and want, and now you can even feel freer from the fraught pressures that deprived you of fun.

Find Freeing Fun

When you resolve worries, you can more readily find fun and be in that fun without your negative, worrisome thoughts contravening.

Finding freeing fun is essential to letting go of the thoughts and worries that have been running you to enable you to enter a joyful state of being.

If finding freeing fun is something that eludes you, go for a walk and let yourself remember times when you were laughing a little or a lot; times when you were alone and felt an inner, energizing joy; times when you spontaneously switched from what you were doing to play. Perhaps the latter was playing with a pet or child. Children and dogs are wonderful beings to help you let go so you can be fun.

The ordinary English expression is "to have fun." But is fun a thing you actually *have*? The word "have" has several meanings and chiefly means to hold in possession or acquire or possess. But you can't acquire or possess fun. You experience it. It is a state of being. Usually, it comes spontaneously. You can't put it in a plastic container and open it when you need it. If a comedy you watched was funny or, at work, you laughed with a coworker, you can't necessarily repeat the experience. If you watch the same show, the second time you're bound to laugh less. The third time you may not laugh at all. If you have some free time at work, you can repeat what initiated the fun and laughter, but using the same words may just result in a strange look from your coworker. Even so, if you keep finding fun as a conscious focus, you can find it in unlikely places. Here are a few, which we'll look into:

- Talking to a cashier can be fun.
- Preparing meals can be fun.
- Exercise can be fun.
- Seeing something new can be fun.

- Taking time off to sense your body can be fun.

Fun is also letting go—letting go of your worries, concerns, aches, pains, all your "to do" things clamoring for their time and your attention. Practice giving away all these things that weigh on you. Give them to your higher self, give them to God, give them to an imaginary friend. The point is, while you're being fun, you can be freed of all that is holding you down and back.

This does not mean that you are shirking your responsibilities. It is refreshing you so that you can forge ahead rejuvenated to fulfill your myriad duties to family, work, pets, your dwelling, neighborhood, country, future generations … and yourself. Don't forget yourself. If you are compromised, pulled in many directions by competing demands, and you become more and more frazzled, then weakened, then you are more vulnerable to physical travails. As you let yourself be spread too thin, your connection to your higher self becomes more and more tenuous.

Talking to a cashier can be fun—if you typically scan your groceries, why not let a cashier check you out? Rather than being withdrawn and not present, a give-and-receive of friendly comments with a cashier can be fun. Many cashiers are aware that part of their job is to be friendly. Passing items through an electronic reader for hours may not be much fun for them. Their relief, if they're open to it, is a good interaction with a friendly customer. That's where you come in. With a little awareness, a little practice, you can easily say something nice, or funny, or observant.

Preparing meals can be fun—while buying or cooking ready-made meals can be the right call at times, it can be fun, magical, and nurturing to find in your refrigerator and pantry

what your bodily systems want and then throw a meal together.
It's good to try to tune in to your body and sense what foods
it wants. This does not mean that you are excluding all indulgences—what you may consider an indulgence or wrong.
Remember: moderation. There's a difference between eating
two pints of ice cream after dinner and a quarter cup. Feel what
foods go together, that want to be combined. When your meal is
ready to be eaten, honor it and yourself. Rather than submerge
your consciousness in news, which can be disturbing, or even
reading, savor each bite with love as you look with gratitude at
whatever view you have.

Exercise can be fun—many people hate exercise, shirk exercise, do anything to get out of exercising. Generally, the more
you exercise, the better it feels. There may be a mere difficult
hump to get over at first if you're out of practice. Even acute
back pain can get better with walking and the right, gentle
stretches. In your mind, go over different forms of exercise, such
as walking, running, yoga, weight lifting, tennis, ping-pong, or
pickle ball. Feel whether you are moved to start and integrate a
new type of exercise in your life, or rededicate yourself to one
you used to enjoy. Then include it each week and enjoy it.

Seeing something new can be fun—go outside and sit on a
nice chair or go for a stroll. Begin to notice what's around you.
Look for something you haven't noticed before. When you find
it—a tree, a pattern of leaves, an unusual building—really look
at it, its color, shape, movement (if any), the way light plays on
it. This is your good time-out to relax and take in something
new. Enjoying visual variety while walking and swinging your

arms can rebalance the halves of your brain and be refreshing and rejuvenating.

Taking time off to sense your body can be fun—kick back in a recliner, or lie on the floor, a yoga mat, or your bed. With your attention, scan your body. Feel any tightness or holding or pain. If you feel pain somewhere, or you remember what's been paining you, you can have fun making it better. This is your time off, and you're creating a space of timelessness so that anything can happen.

Direct your attention to the most prominent place of pain, tightness, or need. Know and feel that you are a source of love and send love to the place. If you're moved to, place your hand or fingertips on the spot. You may need to shift position. Apply whatever pressure feels good. Now, you may wish to place your other hand or fingertips on another spot—for instance, cupping your neck with your thumb on the crook of your neck, or the fingers of your other hand pressing gently on your abdomen, pelvis, coccyx, or pubic bone. Imagine your arms as energy jumper cables and your fingers as the conduit points of contact.

If you wish to visualize the energy flowing into the area as light, do so. Whether blazing light, lavender rays, or a rainbow of brilliant colors, visualize the healing, loving light any way you wish. Keep your fingertips or hand on each spot until you feel the area pulsing. You may want to press or massage it a bit. Continue to hold the position until you automatically take a big breath.

Then tune in to your body to know what is the next place that most wants to be touched. Move on to the next place where you feel pain or an aching or a neediness—that is a feeling of wanting a release or attention. Simply sense which hand wants to go to that spot and then where your other fingers wish to touch and rest. While you are touching and feeling that spot for a pulse that will grow stronger and stronger, feel free to move your other hand to a different place.

If you don't feel any place that is painful or needy, be grateful. Still, you can tune in to your body to visualize what may be blocked or need your attention or wish to be touched or stroked or massaged. This is a gift you are giving to yourself, and a practice you can grow with to help your body and yourself be more in equilibrium with your energy flowing well. Further, as you develop this practice, wisdom is growing within you of knowing your body, what it needs, and how your sense of touch can help you.

You can develop an inner sense of knowing what will be fun and then, whenever you sense a possibility of fun, you can initiate or be open to that experience. Being in that fun, in a sense you are freed of time. Chuckling, laughing, carefree enjoyment rebalances your mind and, thus, you return to equilibrium, a little more human.

Allow Things to Arrive in Their Own Time

Our minds want everything *now*. But the world does not run on your time schedule. We are living in a physical world that is subject to the interaction of many known and unknown forces.

How many steps must take place before you buy a bar of chocolate? How much time and how many steps are needed for the cacao seedlings to grow into trees, for seeds to form and ripen, for harvesting, fermentation, drying, cleaning, inspecting, transport, more cleaning, roasting, shell removal, grinding of nibs, and all the remaining important steps of production until your bar is finally formed, wrapped, and shipped on its journey so that you may buy your favored bar of chocolate? What if you find yourself on a journey?

What if you have a chronic condition? When might you get better and even feel good? What appointments, tests, drugs and supplements, and other treatments would it take for the condition to shift, improve, and eventually go away? But then it might improve only to come back worse. You might follow treatment after treatment, focusing on what helps, what makes no apparent difference, and what makes you worse in unforeseen ways despite its positive prospect, and that could be while applying your wisdom. You may come to realize that good health is a longed-for special gift that contains its own changing mysteries as you follow your own journey. Your journey may find you kicking or screaming, with bitter resentment; or following your professionals' prescriptions with resigned good will; or searching for treatment after new treatment with a positive embrace, relying on your God-given connection for guidance. Regardless of the nature of your journey with the chronic condition, when will you get better?

When will you find love? What nature of love have you been lucky to experience, or sought and so far missed out on? Family love, student-teacher love, the love of friends, loving kindness, romantic-sexual love, love of one mind and soul, divine love? Perhaps you have had love, but then it soured as egos overruled. Perhaps you shared a special bond and love with a friend,

but then your friend's or your dark side reared its head and
the friendship shattered. Perhaps you give yourself a treat, an
adventure—travel to a new city. You make plans to see three
contacts. Two meetings don't materialize, and when you have
coffee with the coworker who moved away three years ago,
the conversation is superficial, stilted, and you leave feeling
estranged. On your last night you have dinner alone, and the
server smiles, welcomes you, and is kind with every interaction.
Love comes when it comes—even from strangers—and can
be appreciated and thanked whenever you receive it. Perhaps
you've been praying or meditating with all the devotion you
can muster, year after year. You know—but can't remember
when—you were uplifted in a swelling of grace, a shower of
bliss, and now the dry spell goes on and on. When will love
come?

Everything forms, ripens, and arrives in its own time. Learn
to appreciate and allow that. There's much to favor in the saying "Do your best and leave the rest." Better health and love
in all its permutations may be elusive. Life is easier when you
are detached while you do your best and don't impose your
decided stricture of time on what you want to arrive when.

Learn to use your intuition to let things go or to take action.
The challenge is to discriminate when your native anxiety or
impatience rears its head, detach as best you can, and not let
those mental urgencies rule you. The goal is to rise above your
impatience, your demands of time. When you let go, when you
flow with time, you can float along in equilibrium, regardless
of the health, the good feelings, and all the love you want and
deserve. The journey is the main thing—the good intentions,

the sincere efforts, the kindness you give to all those you meet, the grace you perceive, the generosity you give and receive, and (with ego quelled) the love you contribute to each moment, forgetting about what is arriving when.

Schedule Winsome Relaxation

With all your striving and good attempts to improve yourself and also be your best self for your family, community, and the world, you deserve to enjoy some winsome relaxation. Winsome means causing joy or pleasure, very lighthearted. Alternatively, if you've been withdrawn, not doing much of anything, and losing yourself in videos or whatever else, some guilt-free winsome relaxation might let you work out or work through what you need to, so that, coming out at the other end, you will find yourself naturally motivated to engage with "what next."

Try using your growing inner sense of knowing as to when you need winsome relaxation and what it will be. Perhaps it's putting your feet up and flipping through an enticing new magazine; or sitting outdoors watching birds fly, looking into the distance, letting your thoughts wander; or lighting candles and taking a bath with mineral salts; or relaxing on a favored piece of furniture and listening to music you love.

The relaxation is a letting go that allows you to rebalance and recharge. You know yourself best. It's up to you to learn to know what you need and when, and then, while not ignoring your responsibilities, to schedule and take your much-deserved relaxation. Relaxation is the adjustment of a system to a state of equilibrium. This is particularly needed if you have been driving yourself to complete some work, if you have been going at life full tilt, or if you are intensely concentrating on inner work. Relaxation is a letting go.

While you are enjoying winsome relaxation, you may be able to feel your inherent childlike joy and innocence. With your first tastes of winsome relaxation, you may want more. Why not try something different? Here are four more ways to rejuvenate your childlike joy and innocence. Schedule any of them when you feel that the time is ripe and for a time when you can be assured that you won't be disturbed. You might even turn off your phone!

Throw a tea party. Invite yourself—that's wonderful in itself. Or also invite a pet, any number of animals (who happen to be stuffed), an imaginary friend, or a very much alive friend with whom you can giggle. Wear hats or funny caps. Serve a favorite tea (preferably from a teapot) and eat lovely sandwiches and pastries—whatever strikes your fancy.

Read a favorite childhood book or one you never got to read. If you buy one or check one out of the library, find one with illustrations that summon intriguing feelings. You might choose *Ozma of Oz* or any of the Oz books by L. Frank Baum, *Oh, the Places You'll Go!* or other Dr. Seuss books, *Wind in the Willows, Alice's Adventures in Wonderland, Harry Potter and the Goblet of Fire* or another of J. K. Rowling's Potter books, *The Tale of Peter Rabbit* or other books by Beatrix Potter, *The Hobbit*, or *Winnie the Pooh*.

Color in an adult coloring book. Find one that you love— many abound—and buy it along with a beautiful array of colored pencils, porous point pens (markers or fineliners), gel pens, or crayons. Again, pick a time when you won't be disturbed, and let yourself go as you pick up colors you're automatically drawn to, filling in the different spaces, thinking whichever way your thoughts go.

Schedule a time to call a best friend when you can talk as long as you both wish. Ideally, this is someone with whom you can share anything, unburden yourself without judgment, be positive and supportive, and laugh about silly things. If you don't have such a friend or you don't feel like calling someone, call—that is, talk—to your imagined better self or guardian spirit and welcome the chance to speak about whatever you want. Have a favorite drink close by and relax in a comfortable chair or lie on a couch. By the end of the conversation, you should feel lighter, more like a human being, perhaps even a spiritual being having a lovely human experience.

CHAPTER SEVEN

The Five Sources of Wisdom

Clearheadedness
Inspiration
Intuition
Forgiveness
Listening

When you are born, you don't come in with a *tabula rasa,* a blank or empty slate. Because you have traversed your own unique path, having many human experiences of different lives, as well as spiritual and mental growth between lives, you come into this body and life with your own unique mental and moral development. As you grow and mature, who you are and who you are meant to become emerge. You may possess certain inherent knowledge and skills—such as herbal healing or making music—that remain in the background until the space and time is ripe for them to come to the fore. Thoughts about your special occupations may surface from time to time, but the knowing and resolve to pursue that vocation won't come until the space and time are ready and then you can capitalize on the mental impressions that are now accessible.

You have five sources of wisdom. Imagine five inverted

aquifers or wells of knowing that are interconnected in your mind. The mental development that you already possess when you are born has a direct bearing on your ability to develop each of the five sources of wisdom. Your willingness is an important factor that is also preconditioned to a large extent. But forget fate, forget destiny—now, reading this and acting on it is your opportunity. It is not meant to be apparent now, but you have been developing your mental apparatus, your cognition, your higher knowing to varying extents for X TO XXX (or perhaps X,XXX) lives and between lives. You may have a sense of this. Perceptive friends might say, for instance, "Diane is unusually intuitive" or "I don't know how Emma is so easily inspired." Each of these sources and inherent talents or gifts can develop or shut down as you go through life. It depends on what you go through, how you respond, and what you do with what you possess.

You may have a sense as to what brilliant waters run in your wells of wisdom. For now, rather than try to figure out what gifts and abilities you possess or what you could attain, hold the belief and have faith that you have an unlimited capacity to develop all your sources of wisdom, and that now your capacity and ability are more than you can imagine.

As we explore these sources, think of your consciousness as a fertile field that you will till, sow, water, fertilize, and weed, drawing from your wells of wisdom. Remembering to attend to your field is key. Have fun, rest, or relax whenever that's wise, yet also remember to be aware so that when inspirations or intuitions come, your attention is primed and takes full advantage of the opportunity. You can use the Journey Journal you

downloaded or created to keep you on purpose and enable you
to progress more confidently on your journey of recovery and
discovery.

The five sources of wisdom are:

- ➤ Clearheadedness
- ➤ Inspiration
- ➤ Intuition
- ➤ Forgiveness
- ➤ Listening

Clearheadedness

The first source of wisdom is clearheadedness. It may be defined
as being able to think clearly, rationally, and logically. If your
mental state is a constant bombardment of thoughts that are
scattered, hazy, and delusional, it is challenging to access your
wisdom.

Thus, it is crucial to be aware of your thoughts and question
them as to whether they are faulty beliefs based on prejudice,
misinformation, or misperception, rather than facts and truth.
A book could be written on this subject, but the scope here is
to enhance your awareness of the levels of clearheadedness
and steps you can take to foster it. Many people are subject to
blind delusions. They are usually unaware of them because they
subscribe to their beliefs whole-headedly. When they are entertaining these delusions, they are occupying an alternate reality.
Examples of blind delusions include:

- Believing that someone is interested in you when they are not
- Thinking that someone has written you off when they haven't
- Buying things indiscriminately thinking that somehow the money will come to pay for them
- Believing that you are okay when you experience strange feelings or pains and part of you knows it would be best to seek professional help
- Believing that coworkers find you funny when your statements are actually insulting or debasing them

If you experience a glimmering that something is not what you think it is, focus on it, unravel it, and let this be a welcome nudge to apply clearheadedness and discrimination to the situation.

Are You Sacrificing Your Clearheadedness?

You may be sacrificing your clearheadedness in a number of ways of which you may be unconscious or only partially aware. Here are four questions you can ask yourself and explore: 1) Are you under the influence? 2) Are you under someone's spell? 3) Are you compromising yourself? 4) Are you being run by subconscious beliefs?

➢ Are You Under the Influence?

If you are under the influence of mind-altering drugs or alcohol, your ability to think clearly and your intuition may be impaired. To master wisdom daily, you need to be in full possession of your faculties, which include clear and sharp thinking.

You know yourself best. You will need to know the balance you wish to achieve, but also how much you are attached to particular alcoholic drinks and drugs. You may not be ready to take action for months. The key is to know yourself, your goal, and how to best achieve that goal. Is it to wean yourself slowly, go cold turkey, or continue to partake when you feel it is called for? You may know to what extent you should refrain. As you develop your wisdom, tapping into the well that you have and accessing hitherto unavailable sources, you may empower yourself to refrain from drugs and alcohol entirely to be as clearheaded as possible. The goal to strive for is to be aware every day what your clarity and balance are in all things. That is developing your wisdom.

> Are You Under Someone's Spell?

Unbeknownst to you, you may be acting under someone's spell. Close friends and family—those you may love and cherish— may ingratiate themselves to you to get you to act on their behalf. This may not be in your best interest. To be at their level and/or to be pleasing to them, you may be acting in ways that are not the true, natural you. You may be adopting what you perceive as their attitudes and thus feel certain things about yourself that are not true. Thus, this may involve parting with more money than is fair, doing more household chores than is fair, sacrificing your goals and ideals when this does not serve you. This is not a call for you to be selfish. Rather, it is guidance to examine your relationships from a detached, clearheaded perspective.

We want to be giving in relationships. But also: Are you able to discern what is and what is not serving your best interests and to be your authentic self? Freely, naturally, unguardedly, without censor? Naturally, to varying degrees you act differently in different relationships. You act differently around your boss and a confidante whom you trust. The key is to discriminate and be aware if you are acting under someone's spell. You don't want to sacrifice yourself to be what you hope that person wants. You want to be free to grow and develop and master the wisdom of living your life in your own way.

Suggested activity: Make a list of family and friends with whom you are or have been in close contact. Clearly, honestly look at their relationships with you. Are any taking advantage of you? If you have imbibed another's sly dictum about who you are, what you need to do, what you fail to do, where you come up short, or how you should act in various situations, first explore the truth about the situation. If there's truth in any of their views, then your taking corrective action may be the good, wise move. Remember, critics can be our best friends—that is, if the critic is acting from a place of truth and their intention is good as opposed to merely wanting to vent negativity, take you down, or mold you to their view to satisfy their ego desires.

If the views of the particular family member or friend are not true, you need to be wise as to how you handle it. The fallback, unconscious strategy of some may be to ignore the other person, to be passive-aggressive, to take down the other person by criticism, or to sabotage them where they are weakest. This is compromising and lowering yourself. It's wreaking havoc on your equilibrium.

This is where your wisdom comes in—knowing how best to handle the situation. It may be engaging in a polite conversation with the person explaining how you feel while not making them wrong. If the person's belief and behavior is a well-ingrained track that you feel that they cannot free themselves of, the wisest course may be acting the part of the good daughter or son, for instance, and giving what you can and holding firm on what you cannot. If the person is someone you don't have to have in your life, the best course may be withdrawing from that person, kindly, and eventually they may get the message. If the person's behavior continues to rankle you and even rules your behavior, however, you need to find a way to break the spell you've allowed to be cast on you.

You may be acting on a spell that you allowed to be cast years ago, and be unaware of it. Being in certain situations may trigger it. For instance, acquaintances may ask you to give your valued services for free, and because someone you looked up to and deferred to and whose opinion you swallowed first had you act that way, when an acquaintance or friend turns to you for help, not respecting or valuing you, you may automatically quash your self-regard and feel obliged to do that person's bidding, even though you may not want to and that person may not even care about you.

Look back at elders and friends you looked up to, who influenced you, and whom you wanted to emulate. Being aware of their power position, that person may have cast a spell on you to act a certain way to satisfy their ego needs and wants. You may still act in this regard when that spell is triggered. This may be especially true if you looked up to the person in the context of a religious or a spiritual group. Or it could have been someone advanced in the profession you wished to advance in and they took advantage of their position of power.

> Are You Compromising Yourself?

Webster's definition of compromise is "a committal to something derogatory, hazardous, or objectionable; a prejudicial concession." Thus, this may be a compromise of character, where you embrace something derogatory, objectionable, or hazardous. It is turning away from the best you—the you that, when you express who you virtuously are, makes your heart feel full. Further, the best you is free. Now, you may think that being totally free may lead some people to express themselves disruptively, dangerously. But we are aiming toward wisdom and the ascendance of your higher mind, so that unkind outbursts—expressions that do more damage than good—are sublimated and redirected to something constructive.

There are three main ways you can compromise yourself. You can compromise your character, body, and equilibrium.

Your character: There are multitudinous ways of compromising your character. First, look at your interactions with others. You compromise your character when you gossip, lie, cheat, or take down another, and when you indulge any negativity, including judging another. We make assumptions about others, then judge them when we *don't know the full truth* about that person. You can know yourself better than anyone. When you go along with someone's lower impulse, using whatever justification comes to mind (or none) and ignoring the subtle or urgent whispers of your conscience, that is compromising yourself. If you attend to your conscience and focus on clear thinking, this is where wisdom can come in and rescue your better self. Also, developing your will and expressing it appropriately is a way of strengthening your character and not compromising yourself to your detriment.

Your body: In a real sense, your body is a temple of the living God. You are compromising your body when you rush, pushing to get things done, and when you deprive yourself of needed sleep to work as long as you can or to keep watching or playing—anything to absorb your attention. You compromise your body when you provide services in ways that don't support your health. You compromise your body and your character when you have sex because you believe merely that you should, or to advance in your profession, or when you let lust take you to places that obliterate your better self.

When you compromise your body in such ways, you impair your finer nature. Along with the physical fallout, your ability to think clearly is muddied. Further, the will of your higher self is weakened. Finally, when you compromise your body, you lose your way in any number of regards. Your body is the physical locus of your spirit and mind. It is your *selfship* in which you are journeying through this world and present life. To navigate treacherous waters, to negotiate with, resist, and overcome foul-minded people, self-appointed admirals, and pirates who would commandeer your vessel, you need to keep your body in shipshape condition and be vigilant and clearheaded.

Your equilibrium: The four main ways you compromise your equilibrium are by:

- Negative thinking

- Taking in negative speech, writing, or actions of others firsthand
- Taking in negative news or media
- Holding self-compromising beliefs

Negative thoughts and strategies to neutralize them have been discussed previously in different sections. When you take in negative speech, writing, or actions of others—especially when it is directed at you—it is easy for it to become imprinted as a streaming, repeating tape of negative thoughts. This includes the actual negative expressions, your mind's variations as they are repeated, and your imagined responses. For instance, some-one might tell you with a negative spin, "You're a good one." Hearing this, different mental imaginings and judgments of how you're not good enough can run through your mind. If you don't know what they meant and ask about it and they put you off, this can further entangle you in their icky web.

The more intense and negative the negative expression, the easier it is for it to get deeply ingrained. Until it is resolved or released, your equilibrium is shattered as you continue to get upset or disturbed. If it feels safe and hopefully productive, you can arrange to communicate your truth lovingly to the offend-ing person or persons. This can resolve the issue and dispel that negative track. Otherwise, you can practice a means to release the negativity to return to your spiritual center. This may take a varying amount of repetition and a strong will, and you can succeed.

Positive and spiritual experiences, on the other hand, need to be focused on, savored, and remembered again and again to become embedded in your memory. It is a shame that a beautiful, uplifting experience can turn into a wisp of a thing, then escape your recall, while a mean, cutting remark can play over and over, quaking your peace of mind, making a groove in your mind. But that is the nature of most minds and why taming your mind and making it a good friend can easily be a lifelong project.

If you are committed to maintaining and returning to equilibrium whenever you realize it has been upset, then it is important to be on guard for negative news and media. Violence, catastrophes, natural disasters, fighting people, angry words that you watch or hear—no matter how removed—can similarly become lodged in your thoughts. As they replay, this triggers fear or anger. Therefore, while wanting to stay informed and be entertained, it is important to choose news outlets and entertainment that won't be disturbing and from which you can be best detached. That way, not having negativity revolve in your head, over and over, can be as easy as turning the device off.

Self-compromising beliefs can be tricky and ever so sticky. These can be beliefs that became ingrained when you were a child—beliefs, for example, that you are fat, unattractive, unconfident, dense, incompetent, weak, stupid, needy, apathetic, or helpless. When you are aware and unaware that you are thinking thoughts that are expressions of these and other self-defeating beliefs, your equilibrium is compromised. Something is not right—or good. There is tension in your self-image and/or how you relate to others and the world. Thus, your behavior will reflect a lack of positive self-regard and synchronization with who you admirably are. You are indescribably better than these self-defeating beliefs. But what if you are not conscious of them?

➢ Are You Being Run by Subconscious Beliefs?

The answer is most likely yes. This is one of the trickiest and most subtle ways in which you are being kept from achieving your optimal clearheadedness. The reason is that you are unaware of subconscious beliefs unless you have released them. Releasing them is one of the most important ways to facilitate healing—mental, emotional, physical. It will release the impediments to accessing your true well of wisdom, rather than being run by your lower mind's propaganda machine. If you suspect that you are being run by subconscious beliefs, you may decide to accept this as a project and find a professional or a means to allow you to release them and heal.

Levels of Clearheadedness

As you work with yourself, you can gain keener clearheadedness and enhanced knowing.

To better understand clearheadedness, we can examine its five levels. These levels are intermittent, cognizant, intentional, developmental, and master clearheadedness.

❖ Intermittent Clearheadedness

Intermittent clearheadedness is simply when clarity comes at times of its own accord. Going about your day, clarity may flash through in thought, feeling, or expression. It may address a good way to complete a project that had previously eluded you. It may be an unexpected knowing of a course of action you need to take. In a flash, you may see a friend or coworker clearly. It's as if a veil was lifted and now you understand how they probably feel, what their true motives are, and/or the quality of their character.

Think of a perfectly clear glass, a clear day you awake to, a clear feeling of gratitude, knowing, purpose. This may give you a sense of the experience of clearheadedness. When you begin to pay attention to your flashes of intermittent clearheadedness, you begin to attain the next level, that of cognizant clearheadedness.

❖ Cognizant Clearheadedness

Cognizant clearheadedness is when you are aware when you are being clearheaded. You acknowledge it and you begin to truly appreciate these instances. As these occur more often, you begin to want more instances of clearheadedness. This leads you to intentional clearheadedness.

❖ Intentional Clearheadedness

A good example of when you try to experience intentional clearheadedness is when you have a situation about which you want to take action, but what action to take has been eluding you. You may have been weighing different options with their confusing pros and cons, or you may not even be aware of the different courses of action. Seeking clearheadedness with intention, you would then turn to what you sense are the best means of achieving it. Remember when someone is faced with a problem, they are getting nowhere trying to solve it, and then they say, "I'll sleep on it"? In some instances, that may work as a means of the solution rising to waking consciousness. While they sleep, somehow unbeknownst to them, their mind sorts out the situation and the next day, at some magical moment, the appropriate course of action becomes known to them.

Intentional clearheadedness is when an issue—oftentimes one you've been postponing—comes up again in your mind and now you feel: this is the time to deal with it. And you use the means that best can deal with it. Whether or not you've tried sleeping on it, these may include writing out the pros and cons, mind mapping or intuitive clustering, meditating, intuitive sussing, taking a rest from trying to figure out what to do and knitting, or taking a walk, playing with a pet, or other recreation. Eventually, the course of action clarifies in your mind. As you continue to practice intentional clearheadedness, you may know your mind and yourself better to the extent that you know what helps you to achieve clearheadedness.

If you lack confidence in yourself to negotiate life and you have an inverted ego—that is, a negativity that belittles your innate worth and abilities—you may have formed the habit of asking others for advice. But others simply don't know you as well as yourself. Unless they are perfectly empathetic and wise, they will give you advice from their subjective perspective. Further, friends you turn to for advice may not have your best interests at heart. If you need to ask others for their opinion, pay close attention to what they tell you, and when you are alone, engaged in an activity in which clarity can come, see how their words serve you. If you realize that they don't have your best interests at heart and may even be antagonistic, if they are in your life and out of habit you find yourself still asking for advice, then you may realize that doing the *opposite* of what they propose is in your best interest. Still, with your awareness of your growing abilities, you may decide to turn away from seeking advice from outside you so as to develop intentional clearheadedness by relying on your higher knowing. Thus, with practice and faith, you may graduate to the next level.

❖ Developmental Clearheadedness

Developmental clearheadedness is when you continue to be aware of the value of clearheadedness and the benefits it concurs and you apply yourself to achieving it as a more regular state of consciousness. This includes consciously going through experiences and forming a clear understanding of their outcomes, their impact on you and others. Thus, when you reflect on an experience, you can learn from it. Even if you repeat "mistakes," by continuing to reflect on the experience, you will eventually embark on the experience with clearheadedness and now usually achieve a favorable outcome.

The means of pursuing developmental clearheadedness would be individual because you have experimented with various means of achieving clearheadedness and you continue to be cognizant of what works best for you when. Thus, if you have work situations that you need to think through clearly, you may have found through experimentation and experience that swimming laps best helps the competing ideas, impulses, and dross fall away to arrive at the optimal course of action. Here you have gotten to know yourself better and taken responsibility for the atmosphere and workings of your mind and what best develops clearheadedness. As you practice more and more and achieve clearheadedness through whatever means—applying it with your good knowing to different situations—you begin to attain master clearheadedness.

❖ Master Clearheadedness

Master clearheadedness is when most of the time you are clear-headed and your knowing is usually automatic. There are many degrees of master clearheadedness and your mastery of it is enhanced as you continue consciously to attain that state and live in it. When you have mastered clearheadedness to some degree, you have a lighter touch about life—because it's easier and more fun. Negotiating challenges is less fraught—because you know what to do. You don't have to equivocate for days and hours on end on decisions—you make them easily when the time is ripe. You are living on a higher plane. A certain joy pervades your waking hours—because you are living in your wisdom, your growing wisdom.

Inspiration

Inspiration is a breath of fresh air that rejuvenates and renews your being. Its soft, welcoming breeze brings fresh ideas and energized motivation. Inspiration comes when you least expect it.

The word "inspire" was originally used of a divine or supernatural being, in the sense of to impart a truth or idea to someone. Inspiration is related to "spirit," which comes directly from the Latin *spiritus*: a breathing (respiration, and of the wind); breath of a god, hence inspiration; breath of life, hence life. Remember, you are spirit and the divine is *within* you—your soul. Your soul is a particle, a ray, of the Oversoul, call it what you will. The soul is part of the creative force. The soul is that which animates us. You can also think of inspiration as new life. Your higher mind—your nobler, better mind—is more receptive to the soul's influence than your lower mind.

What are the sources of inspiration? There are three that vary in frequency and commonality from person to person and also at times in your life: inspiration from your higher mind, the experience of love, and the experience of oneness.

You can't make inspiration happen. Inspiration comes unbidden. It can come while you are brushing your teeth, while you are looking out a window and daydreaming, while you are meditating, while you are walking to another room or rinsing out a cup—at any unexpected moment. These can be moments when your overactive, chattering, worrying mind recedes and a knowing comes through to your awareness.

As a source of wisdom, inspiration delivers an immediate knowing as to how to surmount barriers, where to direct your attention, and "what next." What next can be what you do next in a creative work, like a painting, or a next step in a business endeavor. It may be a definite expression of what was heretofore in the background and now that bolt of inspiration crystallizes it into clarity. The inspiration may be unarticulated thought—so that you automatically move on to what next, enjoying and grateful for what can be likened to a divine infusion.

You may have the ability to inspire yourself. This may develop and come into your life as you continue to achieve equilibrium and master wisdom daily. You may facilitate inspiration by feeling positive, by reveling in the unity of nature, while meditating, by engaging in quiet selfless service, or by connecting with another in a field of truth and mutuality.

Intuition

Intuition is direct, immediate cognition and spiritual perception. *Webster's* defines intuition as "the act or process of coming to direct knowledge or certainty without reasoning or inferring : immediate cognizance or conviction without rational thought : revelation by insight or innate knowledge : immediate apprehension or cognition."

You can experience intuition in many ways. Here are four ways, all of which you may have experienced or you can learn to recognize and develop.

- Intuition may be an immediate, sure inner knowing. Like inspiration, here it comes unbidden; for instance, when something is not working and you realize you need to stop or you need to do something now, like call someone.
- Intuition can be something you suss out by asking questions of your higher self, your sense of higher knowing. These could be yes or no questions. Or you might be seeking an answer to a comprehensive situation. The process may require you to follow a line of questions, using your immediate cognition as to whether what you ask is true, yes or no, or to what degree it is optimal. Perhaps you're debating whether to go on a certain yoga retreat. You could ask for example: *On a scale of less than one to ten, to what degree would it be optimal to attend the Bhakti yoga retreat this coming*

June? Is it at least a one? Is it at least a two? Each time you get a "yes" or a strong, positive response, continue up the scale. Typically, you would want at least a seven in degree. When you receive the answer to your question, you can proceed to ask what is the next information you seek. Perhaps you're debating whether to share a room or splurge on a private room. In this way, your intuition may be a series of steps, surmounting one step of knowing after another, until you've reached the summit and know what you need to know, having experienced the surety of truth.

- Intuition can be a strong, driving feeling that automatically translates into knowing; for instance, something's dangerous—you need to avoid it.
- Fourth, intuition can be a subtle feeling, like a hint in the corner of your mind that you need to grasp and which, if you stay with that hint, focus on it, and pull it out until it's vibrant and clear, you may realize a valuable direction or knowing.

In tuning in to your intuition and developing it, a challenge can be in differentiating between true knowing and whispers from your lower mind, the mind that is entangled in attachments and driven by lower passions. This takes practice and knowing yourself better. As you experience knowing what you need to know and that your intuition proves to be true, faith in your intuition will develop and strengthen.

If you wish to differentiate intuition from inspiration, you can do so in three ways. The first is distinguishing them by what they are. One simple way to express this is: intuition is coming to know what is true, while inspiration is seeing where to go.

Thus, in many cases inspiration is giving you a window as to a new idea, a fresh shift in your mindset and spirit, "what next"—at times, a solution to a problem. Intuition is knowing what's good for you.

A second way they can be differentiated is that you can develop your intuition, whereas inspiration comes unbidden. You can do your best to create the conditions in which inspiration may come, but you can't will it. Letting go is important for both. For inspiration, it is most likely to come when your thoughts about the issue are absent. Remain positive, remain open, and occupy yourself with good works to create a welcome space for inspiration.

The third way they can be differentiated is how they relate to wisdom. In bringing its wisdom, inspiration can teach us openness, humility, and the love of wonder. Also, you can begin to value the recession of your ego and learn how best to transcend it or manage it. Intuition can profoundly build wisdom. You can practice intuition, and if you practice it regularly and well, your field of knowing expands to the degree where you know yourself well, you handle your life well, and your knowledge supports your endeavors time after time.

Forgiveness

Not forgiving the presumed faults and foibles of others keeps us from growing in wisdom. We remain mired in the presumed faults of others and in our judgments. Doing your best to try to understand why the person acted the way they did can bring you closer to the door of forgiveness. Most people mean well, and since people are not all-knowing and are ruled by the mind, which can readily express itself in a rush or a calculation of negativity, they can easily hurt other people. But by deciding truly to forgive, you can go to the source of wisdom. By going to that door, opening it, and walking through it, and completely *letting go* of what you hold against the other, you are severing the mental bonds that kept you in the negative head space of feeling hurt, resentful, or any of the other myriad reactions to feeling you've been wronged. You may also come to a more profound depth of appreciating why people act the way they do. You are freeing your awareness to open to and practice mastering wisdom daily.

Holding grudges, slights, and wrongs, you're like Lemuel Gulliver in Jonathan Swift's prose satire, *Gulliver's Travels*, who woke in the land of Lilliput to find himself bound to the ground with hundreds of little ropes affixed by the tiny people of less than six inches—you can't move. Forgiveness is a letting go and moving on. It's a release from the mental tentacles that keep you attracted and attached to negativity, your lower self. Opening your heart to forgive completely dissolves these tentacles and releases you to get on with your better life.

Do we truly know why people (and we) act the way we do? To acknowledge that you don't know the inner workings of the mystery of others can usher in wisdom. It is humility. It is acceptance. With that, comes release and your higher mind is no longer dragged down by your self-righteous hurts, which you love to unfurl and wave to give yourself justification for feeling wronged (which has been letting you feel "good" about feeling bad). *Of course*, if someone *is* hurting you and your well-being is being compromised in any way then, with a detached mind, your challenge is to come to know the best way to handle the situation that will serve you and protect you without indulging anger and retribution. If someone breaks the law, then you have the right to pursue the matter legally to seek redress.

This life is a vast play. By not learning how you can forgive and by not forgiving—instead, hanging on to the hurts—you are, in effect, writing further scenes, wanting justification and justice to keep playing out. The demand for justice will ossify into karmic debts, adding further strata to your aquifer of higher consciousness. Eventually, you will return to play out some of these new debts—later after you have not forgotten, or in another life when you won't know why you and others are enacting the strangest scenes.

Thus, why not realize forgiveness and be released? Do we want justice or mercy? For ourselves, that's easy—mercy. Wanting justice, demanding justice, craving justice creates debts that must eventually be paid. Anger is the fuel that stokes the fire and creates more hurtful speech and deeds. Even with a hurt from years ago, it will come up in your awareness from time to time when you least expect it, and when you chase after it and push yourself through that mirror to revel in that hurt, that injustice, you abandon your equilibrium. Then, when and how can you return to your nobler self?

You succumb to that anger, but that anger has been rankling in the background. It has been compromising your ability to access and appreciate the eternal now. It's there, even though you may not be aware of it. Then it strikes—in unexpected negative ways. In any case, with anger, you're stuck, in disequilibrium, and this is blocking you from progressing further in your evolution to wisdom.

What about *your* transgressions, of which many you remain blithely unaware? How can those be dissolved along with those hurts by others you continue to cling to? A high practice of wisdom is to petition LoveSource and beg for forgiveness for what stands between you and that Power. Remission of trespasses of negative thoughts, impulses, words, and deeds removes the mirrors that you are wont to step through and get lost in the worlds of acting out, acting up, and reacting lavishly. That true forgiveness raises you closer to all-knowingness. That is evolutionary.

Love can be a function of communication, and there may be an opportunity to grow in love when you humbly approach those you've hurt to ask for forgiveness. Communication, sharing your truth with love and without judgment, may serve to resolve and release the hurt you caused or suffered, ushering in forgiveness. If you can forgive wholly, on your own, or through loving communication, you are aligning yourself with the LoveSource. After all is said and done, aren't we here to learn to love? By forgiving wholeheartedly and letting go, you can finally forget, and then in the field of forgiveness, you elevate yourself to a higher plane where now you can listen more keenly and clearly to receive even greater wisdom.

Listening

The fifth source of wisdom is listening. The idea of active listening, applying your best discernment to what you are receiving can elevate you closer to truth and wisdom. Listening has five aspects that each exist in a wide spectrum: listening to nature, listening to the wisdom of others, reading, listening to your intuition, and listening to inner sound.

Listening to Nature

Listening to nature is a form of meditation in which our ego recedes and we merge to an extent with the universal. The sounds of birds calling, trilling, cawing; trees rustling and cracking; dry brush crinkling as you walk; fresh gusts of wind; thunder rumbling—these stimulate your senses and can awaken you to the invisible oneness of the life spirit. Feeling part of these multitudinous, multifarious expressions of the life force, you commune with that oneness, your small self falls away, and ideas come, knowing flows through.

Listening to the Wisdom of Others

People in your life may render wisdom when they speak. It may not be readily apparent to them or you. It may be initially obscure, in its own way a riddle that prompts you to plumb to find the meaning for yourself. Those who have your best interests at heart may be able to render observations that can give you insight or revolutionize your thinking. Be aware of prejudgments you render as to someone's age, education, sex, or status that can lead you to discount or ignore their potential wisdom. As discussed in "Intentional Clearheadedness," when receiving the words of others, it is essential to use your best discrimination as to their truth, wisdom, and favorable application to your life.

The best practice is to listen to those who embody the truth. These are realized Teachers, Sages. This is where you sense and test your feeling of sureness, of truth, and your clearest intuition comes into play. The truth and teachings they impart may revolutionize your understanding of existence and overturn generally accepted conventional beliefs. How to find these rare souls? You search, do your best to follow your path, have faith, be positive, and, ultimately, you are found.

Reading

One activity of listening we might not automatically identify as listening is reading. By reading, you are listening to another's words, hearing them in your mind. Ideally, you have chosen wisely and the writing is honed as closely as possible so that truth can be articulated and conveyed in language. Without leaving your living room, bedroom, or commuting vehicle, you can access the greatest minds and evolved sages the world has known. This is the miracle and the gift of books, including audiobooks. A keen regret that some harbor and nurse is that they were unable to meet and sit at the feet of a great Saint or Mystic. Even though hundreds of centuries have intervened and you don't know Aramaic, Persian, Urdu, or whatever language the great Sages spoke, you may be able to access their teachings and receive their wisdom through their written records or their followers' notes (for better or worse) in translation.

Reading the great Sages of the ages, you may find the same wisdoms in their different writings. They may use different expressions and you may need to intuit clearer meanings that transcend the translations, but this could be a most enriching, valuable enterprise in your life. Those who have gone beyond this frail world to the very source of wisdom are your best teachers.

Listening to Your Intuition

We explored listening to your intuition in "The Wisdom of Attending to Intuition" in Chapter Five. Intuition is one of the key sources of wisdom that, if you are ignoring it, you are missing out on leading a life that is better informed, deft, and rich. Life is replete with challenges and difficulties. You have a gift that can make it easier and save you much headache and heartache, detaching you from what does not work. Thus, listening to your intuition can return you to your focus, propel you to the next best thing, facilitate your life.

If you feel tremulous about having even a little intuition, have faith. That can give you confidence and further you on your intuitive journey. Becoming the best you that you can be is simply taking one step. Then, when you are ready, you take the next one. With an assist from your intuition, you can trust that it will be a good one. No matter, you can learn and advance from each experience. If you've got loads of intuition—if you think you know what's best for those around you—be aware of your ego and beg for humility. Reveling in your ego is an excellent way to shut down your intuition.

Imagine at night, awaking and finding yourself in a country house that you somehow sense is filled with awe-inspiring art, sumptuous furniture, a library of the greatest wisdom books, but there is no electricity. You are in complete darkness. You don't know where you are—seemingly somewhere on the ground floor, but you are afraid to move. A feeling comes—move a hand. Carefully, you move a hand. You touch a waxy thing—a candle. If only, you had a match. But don't you, somewhere? You search your many pockets and, finally, in a breast pocket you find matches. You strike a match and light the candle, and now you can see a little.

You move and find another candle, light it, and continue, finding yourself in a grand saloon. The more candles you light, the more you can appreciate your brilliant surroundings. You find the library and are in awe of the titles. If only you had the time to read everything! Perhaps you do. You light a fire in the fireplace, take down a book that most intrigued you, settle in a red velvet wing chair and are thrilled by what you read. Suddenly, you recognize the strangest impulse and you get up, go to an oil painting of a sylvan landscape, and, sure enough, you can move it aside. There on the wall is what appears to be the controls of a sound system. You turn it on, Program 1 appears, and you choose it. You return to your inspiring reading, and the mansion fills with a glorious melody. You realize what a grand rich adventure life can be. You need only strike one light after another. And then you begin to wake up to a new day, grateful that your intuition guides you benevolently.

Listening to Inner Sound

Inner Sound, also called Sound Current, Word, Logos, Music of the Spheres, Shabd, and Audible God Stream by Sages of all ages is the emanation, creative power, and expression of the Supreme Being. It is the very stuff of life. The celestial Sound Current is coursing through all humans. It is just that our attention is so scattered and our downward and outward tendencies so predominant that, for all intents and purposes, the Sound does not exist. As humans, we have the opportunity to focus at our eye center, listen to the Inner Sound, spiritualize our being, and ascend to the higher, more spiritual centers and realms.

At times when you are concentrated, perhaps when you are reading, utterly relaxed in a quiet space, you may notice a far-away sound in your head on the right side. This may be an echo of an echo of the most gorgeous, soul-stirring force in existence.

If you are drawn to meditate on the Sound Current, you can seek a fully realized Teacher or Sage who teaches this practice. As you listen, as your concentration and your spiritual senses of hearing and seeing are strengthened, you are purified. Repeated listening to the inner Sound Current weakens your lower impulses and empowers your higher mind so that you can more readily access and recognize wisdom. Even when the Sound Current is faint and distant or you don't hear it, listening for or to it with faith in your connection to God can deliver knowing automatically.

Listening to the Sound Current is empowering, ennobling, an evolutionary act. Merging your consciousness in the Audible God Stream and ascending to the increasingly spiritual realms can be your path to achieving a fully evolved consciousness of overarching love and wisdom.

CHAPTER EIGHT

The Eleven Evolutionary Wisdoms

The Wisdom of Being Positive
The Wisdom of Being Present
The Wisdom of Higher Consciousness
The Wisdom of Faith
The Wisdom of Sages
The Wisdom of Intention
The Wisdom of Service
The Wisdom of Humility
The Wisdom of Practice
The Wisdom of Perseverance
The Wisdom of Seeking God

The Wisdom of Being Positive

The more positive you are, the more you are like God, the Positive Power.

That is viable. That is evolutionary.

As humans, we have the capacity to evolve spiritually. Being positive with intention, effort, will, and ingenuity and endeavoring to outsmart the negative, lower mind at every turn (with each seductive whisper and every angry burst) is an ongoing valiant struggle in the process of becoming purely positive. As Rumi said: *It takes a thousand stages for the perfect being to evolve.*

Life can be tough. Each negative expression of your mind makes it tougher. Life can be amazing. Every negative interruption and influence we allow to intrude upon our well-being scuttles this. But we live in a world of duality—the dance of the negative and positive. If you are committed to becoming the best you that you can be, then you will embrace the wisdom of being positive and utilize all the tools you have and find any other tools you need as your life journey progresses. A growing positive life is a life of increasing mental ingenuity, hope, awareness, peace, and contentment.

Have you ever taken an inventory of how negative you are during the day? If you are curious, choose a day or three days and, doing your best to be aware moment to moment, note every negative expression. Note every negative thought, impulse, mental scene, speech, and action, and when you do, list them in a written form or make a verbal record. If you feel like it, do this in separate sections for each type of expression. At the end of the day, review what you have.

Perhaps now, you may look into what tools you have for neutralizing being negative. Here are two simple but powerful tools for being positive.

Before speaking, first ask yourself, "Is it true? Is it necessary? Is it kind?" Unless you can answer in the affirmative to all three, refrain from that speech. If you actually go to the root of these questions, realizing what you don't know—each person's complete past of experiences and consciousness—and accepting how easily you can inflict hurts on others (hurts they may suffer for their remaining days), this practice will engender humility. If done with a sincere heart, it will also absolve you from that down-pulling negativity and its consequences. This is also a favorable practice to engage in when you become aware of negative thoughts. No thought goes unrecorded. It's especially important to use this tool when you are riled, upset, losing self-composure. When we make judgments automatically, say and think negative expressions, and issue declarations on the state of the world, do we really know that this is what we *suppose* to be true, as opposed to what is actually true?

Here is another tool you can use that will assist you in neutralizing negativity and mastering wisdom daily. As soon as you're aware that a negative thought or feeling is buzzing around your mind, swat it away as if it were a harmless fly. Then immediately *absorb* your mind in something positive. While exercising your will and concentration, absorb your mind in what for you is positive, appealing, and engaging: a thought, repetition, affirmation, feeling, or beautiful pictures that you imagine in your mind's eye. This can neutralize the negativity that is wont to pull you away from your best self.

The wisdom of being positive is first that you don't know the actual whys and wherefores of what makes people act and say what they do. Casting judgments and getting involved merely demonstrates your ignorance and embroils you in the passing show, stymying your progress and robbing you of time that could be devoted to your real work. That is time that is lost, unrecoverable. The wisdom of being positive is evolutionary because it allows you to avoid being pulled down and frees

you to focus on the all-important inner work and each positive expression of value that would empower and further your
moral, mental, and spiritual evolution.

The Wisdom of Being Present

God exists beyond time. Your soul is timeless.

The more you are fully in the present, the better you can:

- Be aware of the mind's relentless thoughts and rise above
  them
- Appreciate life
- Access your higher knowing

When you are positive, it is far easier to be present. When you
are present, you are more easily aware of the all-pervading,
renewing, loving Presence.

The Presence is available to everyone because each of us is
connected to the Presence. With your attention focused at the
seat of the soul (your eye center), your spirit can open, expand,
and feel the Presence around you and within you. Concentrate,
relax, let go. It is a sense or feeling that is loving, charged, peaceful, alive, and with you. You need never feel alone with the
Presence available to you always. You can embrace this as your
own new now.

The wisdom of being present is that the more present you
are, the more accessible is your wisdom. The wisdom of being
present is that the more present you are, the more focused and
available is your will power. The wisdom of being present is
that the more present you are, the better you can evolve until,

ultimately, the past and future collapse into your new now and can be known to you.

On this journey, you can take things slowly. Be kind and generous to yourself. Your mind is a mighty foe. You have been tricked into believing that you are your mind and its endless, demanding desires. When it is not replaying the past, it is believing it can create the future or fretting about it. All the time, you are dancing to its tune. However you can be reminded, let yourself be aware of your mind's constant pulls and tricks. It wants what it wants, and that may not be good for you. Life goes by quickly when you are caught in the clutches of time, trying to satisfy the demands of each day and your desires. The false urgencies of time keep you from making best use of your life, this vast gift you have been given. Find your best and favorite ways to be in the present so that your appreciation of life can be expressed in ways that further your evolution.

Give yourself the luxury of taking time out to be in the present. Relaxing into the present, your higher knowing can more readily come through to you. Problems and decisions that were whirling around in your head can now present themselves as clear solutions and paths. Yes, being in the present, life can present itself as a clear path—or, for now, a period of waiting, moment to moment, while you attend to what needs to be attended to now.

Life can be simple. It is our minds that make it complicated. Being always at the effect of your mind, you remain embroiled in its agenda, its world. Being in the present, you can begin to clear a path to ways you can evolve in wisdom and knowing to win a richer life, a life that is infused with spirit, a life in which you can begin to see and seek your best destiny.

The Wisdom of Higher Consciousness

At this point, you have likely been working with your awareness, becoming more aware of moments of higher consciousness. You may be developing a desire to live on a higher plane. Your new vision may encompass a vision of a life informed by a higher consciousness, knowing better, more and more, what best to do, how best to be, and what is good for you. You may want your higher mind to be predominant over your lower mind. If you have doubts about your ability to develop higher consciousness, have faith—you have the capacity within you to attain a higher consciousness this lifetime.

This human experience you are having is to enrich and evolve your spiritual being. However challenging and difficult each day is, you can learn to respond with integrity, truthfulness, and love. If you realize you have been pulled away from your spiritual center, you can learn to have faith that your higher knowing can come through so that you know how to return. And you will be able to appreciate the experience of returning to your spiritual center. You are living through one of the toughest schools—this lifetime on Earth. Rather than losing yourself in an escape that buries your higher consciousness or forging heedlessly away in a toxic reaction, you can honor your spiritual being by nurturing confidence in your growing ability to master circumstances because you have faith and growing assurance in your higher consciousness.

The wisdom of higher consciousness is that, in treasuring your life, you make best use of it in moments, minutes, and the months that go by. By allowing yourself to be more detached from the dramas and traumas of life, you can rise above all the down-pulling forces that would otherwise subvert your equilibrium. You can learn to know when to take time out in order to be present and exist in your new now—your timeless moments to rise above the maelstroms of life because the wings of your higher consciousness are extending, showing their strength, and wanting to take you higher.

Higher consciousness energizes your higher mind and gives hope to your soul. If some of the benefits of higher consciousness were to be listed, what might they be?

- Fewer hurtful actions and fewer negative thoughts
- Better appreciation and expression of respect, kindness, and gratitude
- Better knowing what helps and what hinders your well-being and advancement
- Greater facility to be content and happy
- Enhanced awareness of why you are here

The more experiences of higher consciousness you enjoy, the more you will identify with it. Further, you may begin to wonder what evolution to further higher consciousness is possible. And what could that advanced higher consciousness be? To wonder about this can be eye-opening. One of the wisdoms of higher consciousness is that you can have a feeling, an intuition of what exists without actually experiencing that. We are living through an imaginary dream—most of us are unable to imagine or entertain what being fully awake is truly like, what ascending states of realization are. That is why one of the wisdoms of higher consciousness is believing with cherished certitude that there are more things in heaven and earth than are dreamt of in our customary philosophies. Knowing this, you can let this serve as a foundation of faith.

The Wisdom of Faith

Faith is your secret refuge, energizer, and savior that keeps you keepin' on and keeps you open to the realm of seemingly impossible possibilities. When life gets too tough or topsy-turvy, you can turn to that refuge and find faith that things are all right and you can withstand the blows and setbacks of outrageous fortune. In this refuge, you can give up the insistent demands of ego, greed, or attachment to the belief that a power—the universe, God, or your Guru—delivers what you want. Thus, seeking the refuge of faith inculcates humility and, being in your humility (however imperfect), the realm of possibility reopens.

Steeping yourself in the powerfully quiet refuge of faith is also energizing because by humbling yourself you are not wasting outward grasping energies. By finding a posture that demonstrates that you are simply one soul among the infinite infinities of life in all the realms of existence, you are submitting yourself to being chastened, and this humbling act transmutes your receptivity so that grace flows in strengthening you, steeping you with faith and resilience. Thus, you are energized and your spiritual potential refocused to keep following your path, now detached from what may come, but more in tune with your true path.

Finding faith, again and again, is your savior because it transmutes doubt and gives you hope and confidence. Turning within and finding faith in times of trouble restores your receptivity to the renewing showers of grace. Doing your best to find faith is the opposite of throwing the baby out with the bath water—that is, using something you don't like as an excuse to give up pursuing your personal growth, your spiritual practices, your meditation, what you once knew to be true. Unless you and others are the purest of the pure—a realized Saint or Sage— you and others have a dark side that can build and build and coil in its venom until one little incident or remark can make it strike and enjoy sinking its fangs into you or another to poison your clear knowing, thinking, and nobler self.

Believe in the power of faith and your ability to discover and experience it within. Those who pride themselves on being wholly rational and not so naïve as to believe in the existence of God or spiritual experience would scoff at the very idea of faith. What accepted science has proven so far is the boundary of that reality. Let them tread their own path. You are not responsible for that evolution. Rather, if you feel faith, experience it, be grateful, for faith is the immutable flame that you can muster in your darkest hour. It is the gift of grace. It is through faith that we surrender, letting go of expectations and demands, and spiritualize our being. Faith reconnects you to your higher self and God. Faith is the all-purpose antidote to the now you don't want. Thus, through faith, you can emerge in a new now, shorn of your expectations and freed to go forward, whatever may come your way.

The Wisdom of Sages

Humans have a potential that is *vast*. It is beyond our imagination. Never underestimate your potential for mental, moral, and spiritual development. Women and men throughout history have realized their potential to a greater extent than what most people encounter in their lives. You may have studied past Saints and Sages from any number of cultures. They have walked among us. (When the words "Saints" and "Sages" are capitalized, it denotes that they have realized their divine potential as humans.)

Throughout our lives, we receive the benefit of teachers—first our parents, then perhaps siblings. In the years we attend school and college, we receive the benefit of teachers and, at times, other students. When we graduate to work, we benefit from coworkers and bosses who take the time to instruct us. Then all through life, whether it is dance lessons, soccer, painting, football, or yoga, those who teach well enable us to begin to master the skills and what we need to know. Of course, teachers run the gamut. Some have the calling. If we enjoy the benefit of teachers throughout our life, why then wouldn't we need a teacher to help us develop our wisdom and realize our spirituality? Even with these kinds of teachers, it is important to be quietly observant to take note of the operation of their egos and to what extent it is influencing their teaching and interaction with you. The best teachers—the truly rare ones—are those who have transcended their egos.

A beautiful spectrum of sages, past and present, exists, to our benefit. For instance, there have been sages in philosophy, spirituality, the art of living, holy books, schools of yoga, mysticism, and advanced disciples of living realized Sages. With such a broad spectrum of sages and the many purported individual sages with their particular orientations, if you wish to benefit from one or more sages, it can be exasperating trying to figure out with whom to study. But all seeking is good, particularly if you are searching for truth and the benevolent, loving evolution of your being.

Many sages have come to great achievements in learning and consciousness. If you want to study with one, that is admirable. You may want to clarify your short-term and long-term goals for development and evolution, including what, in your soul's heart, you seek. This may be a good time to do some freewriting in your notes or journal. Date it and you can revisit it when you are drawn to and, as you journey and grow, you can always modify your goals. You may be able to identify sages who call to you, meet them, listen to what they share, and even adopt their practice, if they offer one. If you are pulled to search and spend your whole lifetime seeking and nothing fits, that is still time well spent.

You are building a foundation of what fits and letting go of what is not right for you, at least for now. You are also building a fire within you, so that when you come into another life, you can pick up where you left off, and you will possess that inner knowing of what is right for you. As unlikely as it may sound, humans are perfectible and have the potential to realize God. Thus, Sages who have graced our Earth have attained their full human potential—that is, they have attained self-realization, experiencing that their true essence is soul. Some have attained God-realization, having merged their consciousness with God. At this point, they have relinquished ego and triumphed over all the negative down-pulling drives. Being purely humble, they also are powerful and knowing.

The wisdom of sages is evolutionary because first they show us the possibilities of further development. The wisdom of realized Sages is evolutionary because they are living examples of having fulfilled their human potential to evolve. They may inspire you to focus your intention to achieve a consciousness that soars beyond the boundaries of human minds.

If you are intrigued and drawn to find someone who is a complete human, possessing and expressing all the spiritual strengths and virtues effortlessly because that is who they are, you may wish to make a thorough search. If you spend years and years, it is worth it. These complete Sages are the embodiments of wisdom. They are here on missions of mercy to shower their love and give to those who have sought a true life, a surging infinite love, a new now that will exist forever.

The Wisdom of Intention

Intention is what returns you to your path when you get sidetracked, lose steam, lose heart. You may think of intention as your engine that you can turn on by touching the ignition, as you hold the key within you. That key is activating your higher will. Desire is the fuel. Desire to attain the best life possible for you is not enough. Higher desire is not enough—you have to activate and run it through your engine of intention. Intention is to get you over the steep climbs, through the detours, beyond the idling, the stalls, and the diversions.

The world is structured to divert you from forming that higher desire, activating the intention, focusing your attention, and leading your life so that you can do your best to achieve liberation. People might do what they can to avoid suffering and have a better life, but being liberated from suffering *for good* and realizing an all-embracing love is another matter. That is following a mystical path of soul liberation of the highest order. If this does not inspire and pull you now, you can focus on liberation from the predominance of the lower mind. Or if your higher mind is predominant a majority of the time, then you can empower your nobler self by continuing to return to equilibrium, mastering wisdom daily, and becoming more detached from your self-besmirching lower impulses. Reigniting your intention is necessary to keep you returning to pursuing the best life possible to gain your hoped-for evolution this life and beyond.

To better understand intention, you can explore its three elements: your intention directly affects your evolution, your intention is an alteration of your energetic sphere, and each intention is a communication to God. Your intention directly affects your evolution regardless of your perceived success or failure. (Your perception of success or failure is a judgment that can be faulty; being in the valley of where you are today, it only extends so far.) If you are endeavoring to make the best use of your life, doing one thing after another, you might feel that you haven't made a difference, that you aren't getting anywhere. But you likely don't know how you are adding to your foundation, building spiritual strengths and knowing. If you can return to your noble intention—rather than throw the baby out with the bath water—that is the main thing. The mental engagements, exercises, disciplines, and activities you practice are important, *and* the results are not in your hands, even though they may seem to be. Be detached and reengage your intention. Be calm and poised for what's next.

To cite a negative example of this element, someone does something that annoys you and, the next time they do it, you wish that something bad happens to them. It might not occur to you that this is negative. If you pause to consider these wishful thoughts, you may toss them aside as harmless. Here again, you are not cognizant of your intention—to harm another. This intention directly and negatively affects your evolution. It's as if all your thoughts are etched in the sky, then filled in with a permanent marker. This is not our physical sky (with God high above sitting on his throne amidst fleecy clouds). This is etched in your karmic account and will remain there until it is paid off in some way. Now, the tough part of living here is that we don't see the real results of our actions. If we did, and we saw the actual suffering we caused and what we must go through, eventually, to cleanse the etchings, fill them with love, and restore our slate to its pristine brilliance, that would cause a revolution in the way we lead our lives.

The second element to be cognizant of is that the expression of your intention is an alteration of your energetic sphere. As you think, so you are. Each thought, each impulse adds to the sum total of who you are, your being. Thus, negative intentions, mean intentions alter who you are. They don't alter your soul—they encrust it with more crud. This is a key point if you feel a longing (or feel you might at some point in your career of lives) to regain an existence of unalloyed bliss and complete rehabilitated love. Each intention adjusts your being so that you are either better primed or more blocked for greater awareness, wisdom, and openness to positive evolution (and continuing your journey as a human rather than as a lower life form).

The third element of intention that would be good to be aware of is that each intention is a communication to God of where you want to go and how you want to be. Regardless of how conscious we are at this point in our journey, we are connected to that supreme Omniscience. The purpose of the creation is for individual souls to experience seemingly countless lives and forms of life, experiencing separation from the Creator, and after having gone through myriad diverse lives, finally attaining the human form. Then when we experience the longing for that inexplicable, ineffable something that is *missing*, that is the call to begin the return to our Creator.

We try to fill that hole in diverse ways, becoming further embroiled in the world, accumulating karmic debts in life after life. We long more and more for the love that is missing. We evolve—we become spiritualized, purer and purer, and can enjoy the grace to make the journey back to the Creator. Or if your soul is not meant to rejoin its Source, then to continue in the creation, experiencing its mass of diversity until there is a dissolution—a rollback of all life—until beyond time, a new

creation rolls out, creating realms, fabulous worlds and crea-
tures, and universal diversity anew.

The wisdom of intention is to be aware, as well as you can,
of your each and every intention and value its importance and
potential impact on your existence and evolution. Cultivate
feelings of mercy and forgiveness for yourself, likely dominated
as you are by your impulses, drives, and wants. You are a *good
person*. Although you are helpless to an extent—and may not be
aware of your helplessness—still, you deserve the best. You are
one of the One. You may, at times, intentionally or unintention-
ally hurt your fellow beings, *and* you can still embrace the intention and re-embrace it to be kind and loving and intend to grow
in wisdom and humility in your questing for goodness and God.

The Wisdom of Service

If you are one of the One, might others be as well? We all share
the same indwelling Spirit. Another word for God is Diversity.
A trick of this world is to make us believe that everyone and
everything is different. Different bodies. Different thoughts.
Different actions. You have your body, thoughts, and actions,
and since life is tough, who can blame you for looking out for
number one? But by only looking out for your number one,
which you don't own—your body and this life's identity will
leave you one day—you buy into the illusion and miss out on
the *opportunity* to serve.

True selfless service, performed without intention of reward
but with the intention to serve lovingly and do good, induces
humility. In *real* humility, you wear a cloak of invisibility, yet

are risen up in greatness. The cloak of invisibility represents humility that allows you to go anywhere (ultimately), to ascend higher, become closer to and more like the Positive Power. Selfless service is a beautiful evolutionary wisdom. In submerging, loosening, or losing your ego in selfless service, risen up in greatness means that you become greater than your small, boundary-riven self. Thus, this is an opportunity to help fellow living beings, to dissolve boundaries and become more at one with the true reality of ever-present love, and to please God.

As much as true expressions of gratitude flow forth to God and reverberate lovingly within, selfless service does as well. Focused on the task at hand, losing yourself in the good work that serves, you can be in that inner glowing. You can bring about a revolution in your evolution if you approach *everything* as selfless service with the intention and sincere attitude to do your best to please God, while nurturing your awareness of what that means. Thus, you can choose worthy organizations or groups to volunteer with and, if that does not fit into your life presently, you can inspire yourself to go about each task, as if the consciousness of God—that ultimate love and goodness—is within you and you are simply happy to serve and please that Presence. This elevates each moment. This elevates your path. It makes life all the more worth living.

To better understand service and how it fits best in your life, we can look at the five kinds of service: body, money, mind, purpose, and soul. An example of body service is when you help build shelters for the homeless. Money service is, for instance, when you donate money to a relief organization after a disaster. Service of mind encompasses a gamut. It can include volunteering to teach reading and improve literacy. It can be placing in good homes rescue dogs and cats that are in danger of being killed. Mental service can also be reading spiritual and metaphysical texts to discern what is true and can further you on your path.

Service of purpose is seeking and fulfilling answers to the immortal questions: Why am I here? What is my purpose this lifetime? Service of purpose is making best use of your life to strengthen your connection and contact with God. It is wholly honoring the inestimable gift of being born a human, living now with this body.

The circumstances, responsibilities, and challenges you face now may seem pressing. The question of your real purpose is ticking. As the clock of your life winds down, you may now (or later) want with your sincere heart to fulfill your purpose.

First, let's look at your calling. Some persons find their calling at an early age or much later in life and do great things. They may make worthy contributions to the welfare and being of others or to culture. Your calling may be linked to your individual genius. You may have found your calling or not. If not, your challenge is to discern whether you have a calling in the world. You may not. If so, don't beat yourself up and make yourself feel less than. That is dishonoring who you are. If you feel that you do have a calling, but it has eluded you until now, or that you have pursued a particular calling and now it is winding down because you may have another, you can intuit and decide whether fulfilling your purpose is to seek that calling and to discover whether you have a genius that will empower and bloom within that calling.

Whether or not you have a calling, you always have a spiritual purpose each lifetime. In many cases, your spiritual purpose may be out of your hands. When you least expect it, you may be given a life-altering spiritual experience. You may forget it yet be changed. If you remember, you can focus on it, benefit from it, and let it expand into your life. Spiritual experiences often serve to balance the worldliness of your life. Regardless of whether you have a true spiritual experience, remembered or not, you can still fulfill the service of purpose. Keep asking questions and seeking answers about your purpose that will help you fulfill your purpose, express your nobler self, and honor your soul.

If you feel pulled to perform some kind of service but are unsure what to do, look at what you love. This can help guide you to your service. Once you find that service and start to fulfill it, use that love to grow more love and engender humility. Whereas service of money is to lessen our identification with money and help us detach from the world, it is also to help others. Service of body is to help us transcend the boundaries of presumed differences—those of sex, race, ethnicity, political persuasion, class, status, religion, sexual orientation, gender identity, native language, country, region, state, and town. Service of body and mind are to help us rise above these barriers to honor the dignity and deservingness of all, for we are all one of the One, spiritual beings having a human experience. Whereas these services are to further you in all these things and more—like helping to make people happy—they and the service of purpose are also in preparation for the ultimate service, service of the soul.

Service of the soul is upon initiation by a realized Teacher, meditating to awaken yourself to the Audible God Current, the Sound Current. Soul service is the highest form of service and completely evolutionary, for it is incrementally bringing you back, merging you jot by jot, iota by iota with God. This may not be your service this lifetime. It could be X lives from now. The wisdom of service is coming to know what service to devote yourself to and when. It is also to come to know and appreciate the benefits of service. You can embrace the service of purpose as an overriding purpose that keeps your transient journey here up front, something you are grateful for each day you greet and each night you surrender to sleep. It is a wonderful question, an audacious undertaking, to ask and seek: What is my purpose? How can I be closer to God? To rely on your inner knowing, without the prescription of organized groups or leaders is brave and exhilarating. This is truly taking responsibility for your life and your journey of days. It is inspiring humility, for in that humility, all things are possible.

The Wisdom of Humility

Trying to become humble can be a conundrum and a paradox. Humility is the absence of ego. Believing you can make yourself humble; believing that you are humble; thinking that others appreciate your humility are egotism. Humility is the rarest, the most elusive of virtues—it is present when you are not aware of it. To be in the company of a truly humble person—ah, that is beautiful.

A conundrum of humility is if you can't make yourself

humble or even try to become humble, how do you become humble and gain the wisdom and experience of the wisdom of humility? A paradox of humility is while you can't make yourself humble or try to become humble, you can still make realizing humility your heartfelt, determined intention and do those things and be in those ways that *induce* humility; and when it blooms within you and expresses itself, you likely won't be aware of its presence.

To begin to induce humility, first accept that you cannot make yourself humble. You can do your best to manage your ego and it will still puff out its chest when it wants. Ego is the disease. Humility is its cure. Humility is a virtue, a spiritual strength. The closer you are to God, the more you are dyed in the transparent, spiritually brilliant hues of humility. Let's look at four ways to induce humility.

A way to induce humility is to engage in selfless service, especially that which brings you in touch with the needs and suffering of others and allows you to realize your shared humanity. A second way is to engage, alone or with others, in an activity you love during which your predominant ego recedes and you lose yourself. A third way is to return to your spiritual center, through whatever means you have discovered works best. Fourth, meditation can induce humility. In searching for and choosing a meditation, a key aspect to explore is how effective any meditation might be in quelling the ego. Remember, ego is a most tenacious force. Even when your higher mind becomes predominant and your native humility has begun to rise like cream in milk, ego can still ferment your best intentions, spoiling your spirit, thoughts, and better inclinations.

Still, living in an ego-saturated world, what can we do? You can tread your path, following the practices in which you have faith. Nurturing a true, humble heart, you can be alert to the signs that guide you to being and acting in ways that honor the divine in you and everyone. In an attitude of surrender to the wisdom that is available to you, you can turn within. Becoming more attuned to the voice and signals of intuition, you can learn to differentiate between what is so and what your mind is wanting to be so. You can learn to detach from expectations— demands of the mind—and their unexpected sly presentation as intuition.

The wisdom of humility is knowing that you are merely one among almost countless human beings of entirely diverse appearances and journeys throughout worlds of the physical realm.

The wisdom of humility is being grateful for how you are now.

The wisdom of humility is feeling good that you can do what you can and respond however you can to whatever you are given.

The wisdom of humility is realizing that your good efforts are evoking grace for humility to rise in you without you even knowing it.

The evolutionary wisdom of humility is the more humble you are, the more available and attainable is higher consciousness. What is there left to do? Practice.

The Wisdom of Practice

Having never played the instrument, what if you picked up a violin and started playing? The screeches, scratches, and squawks would make neighborhood dogs bark and your family simultaneously beg and bribe you to stop. But if you found a virtuoso teacher and continued to practice (in a discreet place) with great focus and perseverance, your playing could ultimately be inspired and the music from your instrument divine.

You are the finest instrument, and to become your nobler self, you need to practice. What to practice? Here are five areas of focus.

> ➤   Equilibrium
> ➤   Thoughts
> ➤   Intuition
> ➤   Wisdom
> ➤   Meditation

When you sense that you need or it would be good to return to equilibrium, find the time and space and turn to one or more of the ten keys. Unless you know which one, scan the ten keys to achieving equilibrium in the table of contents and feel which one pulls you or resonates with you the strongest. While you engage with the process, allow yourself to freely enjoy it, letting go of thoughts that intrude.

As to thoughts, here are three approaches you can practice to let go of down-pulling thoughts to clear and elevate your mental atmosphere. First, know and remember that *you* are not your thoughts. Witness them streaming through your awareness and be amused at how crazy and persistent they can be. Rather than reacting to them as commands and expressions of reality, view them with detachment. Second, observe and let go of thoughts that stir up negative emotions. For instance, even years later, a mean criticism can strike you again. Simply observe it and let it go. This will pacify your mental atmosphere. Practice being aware of and feeling detached about thoughts that arouse fear, anger, and other negative emotions and letting go of them as easily as you would hang up on a robocall. (It is also important to discern when you need to address a particular fear or anger to know how best to deal with the situation and release the emotion.) Integrate this practice into your day so that it becomes a good, automatic habit. A third practice that focuses on thoughts is to utilize your thoughts to be positive. For instance, embrace the thought and belief: *Slowly but surely, I am evolving into my true nobility.* You have the wisdom to suss out and know which positive thoughts to embrace whenever you notice you are feeling off or not your best.

As to intuition, be primed by being relaxed, in equilibrium, and detached to receive, recognize, and attend to flashes of intuition. This is good practice—having a peaceful mind and opening your awareness. Another area of intuition you can practice is being primed to know when and how your higher consciousness is guiding you. You may have an idea in your head, but then—ah—you get a feeling, to do something else first. Follow it. For example, you may have just completed a task and you ask, *What next?* You think of finding a video, but then you remember something you need to do tomorrow and decide to put out a sticky note or enter it in your calendar. Then you think you'll remember, so you let it go. But then the intuitive urge comes again. Make your reminder.

Rather than rushing and pushing through your life to get one thing after another done, or capitulating to the pleasure or pain you are currently experiencing, be easy and primed and elevated sufficiently to recognize when a sense of something to intuit comes to you. This third way of practicing intuition is when you have a feeling off in the corner of your mind that there is something there, something to focus on and intuit. This could be unrelated to your task at hand and be what you need to do soon. Or it could be an alteration of your submersion in your ongoing involvement that will rebalance you or take care of something that needs your attention. Or, in pain, it could be a door you need to knock on and go through that could lead to the improvement of your condition. You are not alone in your struggle. Rather than feel you need to identify and analyze the source of every goodness, be grateful.

You have been adding to a treasure chest of wisdoms. From time to time, you may feel an intuitive nudge to further develop a wisdom. You may remember a particular wisdom. If you feel like practicing a wisdom, but don't know which one, review the list of thirty-three wisdoms, and sense which one pulls you to focus on it. Or go through your Journey Journal and see what comes up.

Meditation is the great repository of practice that induces the grace to evolve further. It is through meditation, that we can invoke grace, quell the streaming mind, and empower our better selves. If you don't meditate and want to look into it, you might want to define your reason or reasons for starting to meditate and clarify your goals. For instance, you might wish to experience one or more of the following:

❖ Relaxation
❖ Present mindfulness
❖ Bliss
❖ Oneness
❖ Liberation of the soul from the mind

It is important to make a thorough search and not adopt a meditation practice until you are fully mentally, emotionally, and intuitively satisfied that this is the right practice for you. It is through practice that we advance. Practice allows us to get better and evolve.

Each time you practice, whichever focus it is, you can embrace it currently as your wholehearted journey. To prioritize and engage in the wisdom of practice is the antidote to the insistent demands of the lower mind wanting what it wants this instant and taking you away from yourself. To rise above time, we have to go through it in the most positive ways. If you feel disheartened, if you hear the sly, punitive whisper of your mind that *You're not getting anywhere*, then it is time to learn and master the wisdom of perseverance.

The Wisdom of Perseverance

Perseverance is intention in dynamic action. Whatever your practice is, whether you consider it formal or informal, spiritual or humane, occasional or regular, you can approach practice now by leaning into humility, in the spirit of service, with the intention to attend to it with perseverance while maintaining your faith. If you don't have what you consider a practice and you are seeking one, then perseverance is also a wisdom to learn to love.

Imagine that you are exploring a series of caves alone in a foreign country. While you are far from the entrance, an earthquake strikes. Your cave survives, but the passageway out is collapsed. You have no inkling of which of the many passageways you passed through are collapsed. Luckily, you have plenty of water and food (but no cell signal). You wait, being thankful that at least your father knows you were out exploring, but what if he misses the news and does not call the authorities for days? You decide to maintain a positive frame of mind. Rather than sit uncomfortably and pray, you take out your Swiss army knife and do whatever you can to help yourself. With its knife, chisel, and file, you start gouging the rock of the massive slab that filled the opening.

Grains of sand pour out. You keep at it. When your hand and wrist get tired, you switch hands. Rather than pray, asking for and expecting your deliverance, you accept what happened and keep chipping away. Unbeknownst to you, your father has flown to your country and procured a smart bulldozer with a sensing device that can zero in on the sound of your chipping and dig through the earth and rock to release you.

This is our situation. To break through to the light, we must take responsibility to do our best with whatever tools we have and also seek and choose. Then we must practice our practice with perseverance and patience.

If you have committed yourself to a lifelong path, don't give up your practice merely because you feel you are not making progress. Simply engaging with it, by making an effort, that is progress. In the wonderful workings of grace, you don't actually see or know how that grace is furthering your progress when you make an effort. But with a sincere and open heart, you may sense the grace and that may inspire you to persevere with further effort and thus continue to invoke that benevolent circle that is spiraling you higher.

Perseverance is sustained effort with patience. If you have adopted a practice for a trial period or for a limited time, use your discrimination, your clearest sense of knowing to discern whether that practice is complete for now and then "what next" to further your growth. If you are practicing mastering one of the wisdoms, for instance, then (being kind to your self), your goal can be to attend to it whenever you discern the need to develop the wisdom further. Let go of expectations. Enjoy the good work. Be responsible for having a positive attitude and persevering. Let go of results. Remember the wisdom of humility—the more humble you are, the less you are aware of it.

One way to facilitate your perseverance is to integrate it into your life by making it a routine. Whether it is daily meditation or the weekly practice of a wisdom, devote a time and place to it. The mind loves a routine. You can treat your mind—notably your lower mind—as a child. Tell it you know what is best for it and with dedicated practice you will give it a reward. Choose a reward that is beneficial and balancing. The better you observe and know your strong-willed mind, the easier it is to make it a willing friend that won't drag down your nobler self.

The wisdom of perseverance is coming to have faith in your

practices and that your good efforts will ultimately succeed. Change often happens outside of your cognizance. Evolution happens slowly in the quiet, mysterious processes and rhythms of life. Always seek the best for yourself, and all good things you will ultimately become.

The Wisdom of Seeking God

Are you willing to embrace an audacious idea? Here it is: *You can become God.*

Your essence, your soul, is *of* the LoveSource. That is who you are: a lost soul with a divine birthright. Having experienced the creation for XX,XXX,XXX years, are you curious to explore the reality of God?

By seeking God, all good things can be ultimately realized and all your unknowing dissolved—transmuted by knowing. For every step we take toward God, that Power takes one hundred toward us. You may be chipping away at the crud of your mind and, unbeknownst to you, God (or your true Guru) is dissolving the barriers of your aquifer to endless higher consciousness. God loves us to seek our LoveSource more than we can possibly fathom. It is the LoveSource that awakens the longing within us to seek.

You have been on a journey—a seemingly endless journey—laboring under the veil of forgetting. If you had full consciousness of all the pains and pleasures you had endured, *and* just a sense of your true home, that would revolutionize your consciousness.

Seek God and:

❖ Your life is lived on a higher plane.
❖ You are consciously furthering and empowering your evolution.
❖ You are fulfilling your life's true purpose.

Seeking God is the most ennobling mission you can undertake. This automatically aligns you with your birthright, goodness, the storehouse of virtues, and the most thrilling, enlivening adventure. Some people dream of the possibility of visiting the Moon—even Mars—but that is like visiting a barren square foot of rock compared to what happens when you connect with God. If you were connected to the Sound Current and undertook the inner journey seeking God, seeing the surface of the moon, or Mars, would be compared to seeing exceedingly gorgeous worlds of exalted beings partaking of purifying nectars; elevated souls, more brilliant than many suns, singing their devotion to the ever-present Supreme Being; and, as you advance through these higher and higher heavens, ultimately merging, becoming Love, itself.

Let's start with where you are. You may not believe in God. That's fine and understandable, considering that God can't be perceived with physical senses or scientific instruments. Are you curious, though, as to what is possible? Are you interested in: whether you can come to know the secrets of the soul; whether you can realize that your actual identity is soul; how your life might transform if you embraced the wisdom of seeking God; and/or what treasures are waiting for you if, with a true and ardent heart, you seek God?

Seeking God is simply embracing that you are a seeker, after truth, and each day asking what now, what next, and attending to that while you lead a balanced life. To follow this path, you enroll your best intention, attention, intuition, and cognizance. You let go of expectations, judgments, and time frames. You are on a mission of discovery, your consciousness moving toward the Infinite, losing the baggage of many, many lives. Imagine the process for an acorn to sprout and grow into a great oak or a redwood to rise and dwarf the history of countries. Your journey continues and, at some point, you might rise through the welcoming skies of heavens.

The wisdom of seeking God is to challenge time and death itself. It is seeking an overarching continuum that makes your spiritual evolution the top priority. The wisdom of seeking God is to fulfill your responsibilities while putting the demands of the world and your lower mind in their rightful place, thus leading a dynamic balanced life that advances you on your path. The wisdom of seeking God is, ultimately, to transcend time and death and, once you realize who you truly are, to become purer and purer, lighter and lighter, until you are advanced to be one and the same with the One, winning a life that knows no end—only surging Love.

CHAPTER NINE

The Five Prerogatives of Equilibrium

The Calm of Equilibrium
The Commitment of Equilibrium
The Confidence of Equilibrium
The Readiness of Equilibrium
The Responsiveness of Equilibrium

On your journey, this high-level journey that you are undertaking, avail yourself of the prerogatives of equilibrium. These will stand you in good stead as you negotiate the curious byways and people of your journey.

A prerogative is a special quality, a distinctive excellence that accrues as you attain deeper and stronger states of equilibrium. Prerogative is also defined as a special right or privilege belonging to a person. By studying these five prerogatives, you can better know whether you're in a state of equilibrium and this will also help you further develop these states and the place you go to be in dynamic balance. Here are the five prerogatives:

❖ The Calm of Equilibrium
❖ The Commitment of Equilibrium

❖ The Confidence of Equilibrium
❖ The Readiness of Equilibrium
❖ The Responsiveness of Equilibrium

The Calm of Equilibrium

Calm is defined in *Webster's* as "a state or condition of repose and freedom from turmoil, disturbance, or marked activity or from agitation, tension, or vexation." Repose is defined as relief from excitement, danger, or difficulty and also as a place or state of composure or rest. The first prerogative of being in a state of equilibrium is the boon of being calm.

When you are calm, you are far more likely to be in possession of clearheadedness, focus, concentration, and freedom from the myriad bombardments in life that scatter your attention and push you off balance. When you are calm, you can be centered and grounded, and your energy is not dissipating. Your energy is at your disposal. Thus, you are ready and able to respond to what comes up. Some people go through life in an almost constant state of agitation or worry. They're not present to and alert within themselves or clearly observing what's around them. Rather, they're attending to their upset or worry and that, in effect, is ruling them. When you are calm, your mind is in a relative state of equipoise. And you can more readily be present. That is key. When you are truly calm and present, you are also

self-possessed, and that empowers you to make the commitments that you choose.

The Commitment of Equilibrium

Do you know people who never seem to get anything done?
They may look busy. Maybe it's just a lot of sound and fury sig-
nifying not much. You may wonder whether they ever complete
anything, being consumingly busy and making noise. A second
boon of equilibrium is being able to shift at will into a state of
commitment. When you commit to doing something, you "show
up" and go through the steps to the best of your ability to see
it through. Your state of equilibrium helps you monitor what's
happening while you attend to completing your commitment.
Thus, if someone you need to rely on is not following through,
rather than letting your negative emotions take over and rule
how you handle the person, you will be able to remain calm and
suss out the best approach to that person. When unanticipated
delays, discoveries, and problems come up, your equilibrium
will assist you in keeping your freedom in deciding how best
to respond to fulfill the commitment. When something happens
that throws you off balance, if you are in a state of equilibrium
you are far more likely to take appropriate action than merely
react.

To achieve, you need to commit. Equilibrium also supports
the concentration you need to complete the myriad daily activities that comprise your commitments. Commitments may be
formal, unspoken, or organic. A formal commitment is when
you agree to abide by standards or rules. For instance, when you

start a job with a shift or day that begins at a specific time, you make an explicit or implicit agreement to arrive and start work at that time. An unspoken commitment is one that evolves over time so that you are aware of what works and even though you might wish that the reality were different, you make an unspoken commitment within yourself. An example of an unspoken agreement is when you decide internally not to tell your adult children what to do. You've observed multiple experiences of how this has proven to be counterproductive, so now—without verbalizing the commitment to them—you accept what works best and make the commitment to yourself. An organic commitment comes from an amalgamation of input that crystallizes into a commitment. Eventually, with the benefit of experience, you embrace the commitment, for example, to floss your teeth before you go to bed, to take a daily walk, or to pick up the dog poop in your yard every day.

Commitments vary in terms of how conscious you are of them, how involved, what people or things they entail, and other factors. Whether or not you call the previous examples commitments, they are agreements you've made with yourself and they are present in your consciousness in varying degrees according to what else is occupying your thoughts on a particular day. If you find yourself sliding—for instance, spending time on social media at work or skipping walks because you don't like the weather—you may notice that something feels off. Then or later, with your heightened awareness and appreciation of equilibrium, you are more likely to decide whether to marshal your will to correct course, recommit, and follow through.

With every commitment you make and keep, you exercise

and consolidate your willpower and effectiveness, and that builds confidence.

The Confidence of Equilibrium

Being calm and being able to commit to being in a better mental state or doing what's next, what's appropriate, or what's needed helps bestow confidence.

Confidence is a feeling you cultivate when you are in a state of equilibrium. It is a sure feeling, a good feeling, a positive feeling that you are moving forward in your life. You are progressing toward your goals and your life is in a state of dynamic balance. When challenges come up, you can handle them. If you are thrown off balance, you are confident that you can return to your state of equilibrium. When you do return, it's a familiar, welcome feeling. If your confidence gets jarred and you have trouble getting back, you can intuit and remember from past experience what you can do to return to the confidence of equilibrium.

The confidence of equilibrium connotes that you feel good about yourself. You are doing your best. You know yourself better and better. You are aware of areas of your approach to life that need improving and you're working on them. Negative mental patterns are falling away, and when you go to a negative place, you recognize it sooner and can let it go.

The greater your confidence is, the more ready you are to navigate deeper challenges and master wisdom more profoundly.

The Readiness of Equilibrium

The more we mature spiritually, the greater challenges we may be given. At least, it seems that way. Be they health, relationship, money, work, or home challenges, our schoolroom of life seems to advance us to higher grades. This is something we need to be ready for. Thus, when you're in a state of equilibrium and continuing to deepen that state, one of the prerogatives is also being in a state of readiness. When something comes up to which you need to attend, you don't retreat. You are ready and willing. You don't flee from the situation and lose yourself in your favored way of checking out. You don't prevaricate or indulge in a substitute activity. You address it at an appropriate time with a calm, confident state of mind.

If you feel beleaguered—beset with too many demands and feeling that already you've done too much—you can observe this with your growing wisdom and realize that you are not in your optimal state of readiness. And you can realize that you know or can figure out what to do and how to be to restore your equilibrium. With your restored equilibrium, you gain the prerogative of responsiveness.

The Responsiveness of Equilibrium

A distinctive excellence of being in a state of equilibrium is that you can respond to situations more competently than if you were imbalanced, upset, scattered, or in any other state that characterizes disequilibrium. The boon is that you can respond with intent and focus rather than react in a way that has negative repercussions, or withdraw and lose yourself in an escape that sucks your awareness from your better self.

Another aspect of responsiveness is that, as you master wisdom daily, you can marshal your wisdom in responding to a situation, an emotion you're experiencing, thoughts you're dealing with, and people. Each time you marshal wisdom, you can better draw on your experience, intuition, and understanding of people and the forces at play. Thus, an awareness of these factors is growing. Rather than reacting impulsively, you are consciously moving into your response with the benefit of your experience, intuition, and understanding.

Another benefit of the responsiveness of equilibrium is feeling good and using feeling good to shape and enhance your response. Ultimately, you have to practice and teach yourself how to tailor your response. The following can shed light on this.

Being present with yourself, you align your response with a good feeling. The good feeling can be characterized by a calm mind, positive outlook, quiet confidence, and/or readiness to address the situation. Even if you need to respond to a situation you wish was not there, by drawing on your growing spiritual maturity you can accept that a response is necessary. By shaping your response in a positive manner, a good feeling can accompany your response, infusing it with love, knowing that it is necessary. An example is when a parent has to say no for the benefit of their child. Knowing the child and what works best to inform their behavior, no matter how strict you need to be, you can respond to your child's behavior with love and the good feeling that you are helping your child to mature. And this can be done while remaining centered in your equilibrium.

The more adept you become at responding with all these positive forces present, the more natural and effective your response will be. Eventually, it can take seconds. Ultimately, it will be automatic. If you keep engaging with the path you've chosen to empower your nobler self, one day, one sublime moment, you will realize that you are a new you—actually, the truer you that has been there all along.

CHAPTER TEN

A New You

Your Nobler Self

While you have been reading and perhaps practicing with this book, you have been connecting with, being with, and empowering your nobler self. If you have kept a Journey Journal, this may be a good time to go through the early and midway entries to read your freewriting, questions, observations, and insights. Then see and acknowledge how your experiences of being have evolved. Also see whether questions and challenges have been satisfied. If they persist, you can come to know when and how to focus on and resolve the ones that are most claiming your attention. With their resolution, doubts and second thoughts fall away and you are further mobilized to be your nobler self.

You can trust, nurture, and choose to live more as your nobler self. Summon your knowing and trust that you have unlimited potential to realize and be your nobler self. Trust that you have the wherewithal to continue to empower your nobler self day after day and situation after situation, regardless of negative expressions of your lower mind and those of others. Trust that your higher mind can and will let you know what thoughts, expressions, and actions are of the higher mind.

Nurture your nobler self by being accepting, loving, and forgiving of yourself, especially when you screw up or are negative. Previously, you might not have noticed these lower expressions. Allow inputs that will feed your nobler self rather than arouse negative emotions such as fear, anxiety, and anger. This includes videos, shows, social media, and people when possible. You can protect and nurture yourself by remembering to be as detached as possible and encouraging this when a welter of negativity assaults your attention and positive frame of mind. If this spewing energy is a person fuming, remember that they are not their mental explosions, nor need you absorb any noxious emissions.

Choose to strengthen your nobler self by being alert to negative thoughts, questioning their validity and replacing them with positive, forgiving thoughts. Choose to express your nobler self by choosing what to think, say, and write that is of your spiritual core. Choose and cultivate humility. When you let go of the self-important flag-waving "I," around you a beautiful space emerges. This space is inviting of finer experience because of the fragrances of your better self. Also, it allows you to express yourself on a higher plane, more lovingly and truthfully. Better, truer words can come through and you express yourself more authentically.

Your lower self, with all its seductive impulses and indulgences, is readily and easily the place to go. Your nobler self is a seedling that needs ongoing nourishment and training to grow, bud, and bloom. It is a matter of being aware, choosing smartly, and making corrections.

If you were able to know now, while still in your body, the things you have done, the hurts you inflicted, the fear and loathing you caused in your past lives—and even this one—you would be shocked, sorry, and humbled but also grateful for who you are now. You, your abiding consciousness, has been captive to the caprices of your mind. These caprices have generally been indulged mindlessly—that is, without concern or estimation of the results of your actions, words, and thoughts. Now, you have been invited to live on a higher plane, to sow and reap the fruits of your spirit. When all is said and read and done, don't you just want love?

The Path of Love

The movements and experiences on the path of love are unique for each of us. Ideally, it is a path of seeking truth, growing awareness, and becoming a pure expression of love—that wondrous spiritualizing that comes with living with the grace of a focused intention to advance on your path of love.

We can express different types of love. The following focuses on love as oneness. Loving yourself is honoring the divine self within you and caring for yourself in light of this knowing. Honoring the divine within others heightens your experience of the oneness of love. The whole planet is pulsing with divinity. You may be at the state where you can feel it or actually see it, or not. Regardless, never think of yourself as less than. Never judge where you think you or others are spiritually. Rather, embrace your journey as a path of love. What does this mean?

First, each of us is unique with different circumstances,

mental patterns, buried beliefs, and demanding desires. Yet each of us has that perfect love within us. This is our commonality. It's just that our minds, our egos, are adept at smothering it. The love within you is waiting to be found, nurtured, realized, and expressed. This is an invitation to begin to see the illusory nature of the world around you while your main focus is becoming the love within you. Your abiding love—that is your true nature.

How to live it? Go about things s l o w e r than you normally would. This will aid you immeasurably in maintaining your focus. Be aware of being aware and, before and while you do something, remember God, LoveSource. Redefine and reimagine success and contentment day by day, year after year, experience following experience to be that love is blooming within you. When you are not sure about something, ask your higher self: *What would Love do? How would Love be?*

Have faith that you will be provided for. Trust that whatever challenges may come, with grace you will summon the resources to deal with them. Banish worry from your thoughts. And if and when you suffer, embrace this as an opportunity to access your higher knowing, marshal your will and resources, and know you can pass through that suffering and even see how it can be grace. Once you realize you've passed through that suffering, regardless of whether you may seem diminished in some respect, know that love has grown within you. You have advanced on your path of becoming a truer you. Remember, you have an unlimited capacity for growth, for expanded awareness, and love.

In reality, even when we're not suffering, when our attention is ensconced in something else, we are suffering. That is because our soul is longing, longing to be one with the ultimate expression of love. Why are we here? Aside from fulfilling the debts of this lifetime, we are here to grow in love. Love transcends all. Love is beyond boundaries, beyond limitations. You become a new you each moment you consciously know love. This is the path that is available to you. You can do your best to follow your path of love, asking to be receptive to grace at every bend you encounter and every fork, quandary, misstep, and perilous allurement. If you fall, if you succumb to meanness, you can always return to love. That is the joy of becoming.

The Joy of Becoming

The joy of becoming is making best use of your life now and now and now. It is being aware, moment to moment, being in and coming from love, and knowing, keeping the faith, that you are evolving and becoming joy. Yes, you have that possibility, that capacity.

This does not mean that each time you meet someone you whitewash them with the sticky cheer of a hyped-up infomercial gabfest, flashing your blinding white smile of over-bleached teeth, ignoring your authentic feelings, oblivious of theirs. No, the joy of becoming is an inner, discreet experience of gratitude and awareness.

The joy of becoming is without expectations. You are simply doing your best and leaving the rest. Leaving the rest is allowing your process to proceed, unimpeded by judgment, implanted desire, and your attempts to force a sought-after reality into being. If you would like an identity, then you are simply a seeker in the process of realization. Aware that you are to varying extents bound by time, mind, and an impending death, still, you value the precious gift you have been given in this great school. Some students go through class after class without paying attention. Rather, they let their attention be pulled this way and that by pretty people, texts, and posts, or they're hunkered within themselves in a maelstrom of thought. Students who succeed pay attention, listen, take notes, and study. Each day in life, test follows test: where is your attention, are you rebalancing, are you being kind, are you satisfying your commitments, and where is your love? As tiring as it may seem, you need to show up. And engage. Then do your best and let go.

It is more an awareness of being where you are now and being content with that, not resisting, but being committed to becoming your best self. Having faith that you are becoming—that is grounds for joy! Let yourself practice the wisdom of asking questions. How are discoveries made? More likely, questions were asked, small discoveries were made, and that led to more insightful questions. Knowing yourself, you can be realistic about your needs and wants—what it takes to be balanced so that you can focus on the higher priorities of your life. As you evolve, you are better able to choose where to place your attention. Remember, attention is your greatest resource. An irony may be that becoming is so subtle, so fine, you are not aware of it. That is good. Why trumpet it?

If you had to choose between receiving kudos for your achievements or goodness itself, what would it be? If you had to choose between being an amazing star across the social media firmament and being able to shine the light of awareness throughout your day, which would it be? If you had to choose between having so much wealth that you can't enjoy it fast enough and spiritual wealth you will actually take with you, which would you choose?

The seeker's path is quiet and charged. It can be daunting, dumbfounding, and also daring because you are being challenged to access and rely on your best intuition, your highest sense of knowing, and to express your best, your nobler self. As you are becoming, you are growing in spiritual maturity. If you could see now all the past lives you have lived—the families, the hardships, the slipups, and the *growth*—you would be filled with awe. The journey, which you may presently frame as being from your single birth to death, is unimaginably grander. Right now, you may be in the very process of returning to God. If not, you may be preparing to undertake service. To become the best you can be and to grow into a place in which you can truly help others and render service, that is a noble calling indeed.

As you live and discover the quest of becoming, your energy and joy are being transmitted to others in a quiet, powerful way. You can be an unobtrusive model and others may or may not benefit from your good example. Along with the cultivation of the thirty-three wisdoms, you can be cognizant of the gifts that dedication to the path of becoming confers.

The gifts come when they come and you may be cognizant of them, or not. The most sublime gift is grace. Grace is difficult to define and often too elusive to recognize. Because of your good effort, grace may be showered on you in a way that helps you, makes you more cognizant of the sweet prerogatives of God,

and eases you along your path, removing obstacles and infusing you with renewed hope, confidence, and good will. You
may hold grace as that which brings you closer to LoveSource.
Grace is the gift your best effort (without expectations) invokes.
As you progress, becoming more spiritually mature, you can
often sense and appreciate the grace you are receiving and be
grateful. Being grateful is being full of grace. Grace is mysterious. It is the elusive spice that some of us long to have sprin-
kled—or poured—over our life. So, long for grace, crave grace
if you have that inner pull and, more important, do your best to
be deserving and receptive of it, for receiving grace is a glorious
gift. One of the greatest gifts you could hope for.

Grace may bring another gift—faith. Faith is the light in your
darkest hour of need. Faith gives you courage, resolve, confidence, surety. Faith is the antidote to the subversive thoughts of
the wayward mind. That is a gift. When you live in your faith,
you continue to be guided. When you seem to lose your way
and reinvigorate your faith, it can be an alchemy, helping you
proceed on your way, with joy. Much joy can be found in faith.
The world can keep on being crazy, getting unbelievably weird,
but you know your way. You can keep on following your path
of love. For when you least expect it—a turn on your path, an
unexpected exalted feeling, an insight, the dawning of clarity—
you have wonder.

Wonder is the very stuff of life. It is the promise and the
reward. Wonder is what makes us quiver with life. It transforms
us with awe. Wonder can be found in the unlikeliest places and
thus can be an unexpected gift. Wonder is the best-kept secret
of your becoming. Wonder is like a graduation gift you would

never dream of—you'd be too humble even to think of it—but then upon graduation you are given a key to a new kingdom. Never stop doing your best to become. Worlds, actual spiritual worlds of wonder await you. These higher realities exist. As they are less matter and more spirit, you may not be able to access them now, but you can learn about them from those who have traversed them. When you realize them, you are there without your physical body. Your journey can ultimately take you to these worlds of wonder and your being can expand into fields of joy that beggar description.

With your gifts and capacities of attention, wisdom, and equilibrium, you can focus on becoming that joy and ultimately winning a new now that shines forever.

Acknowledgment

This is to acknowledge you, who are reading these words after spending time with this book. Your willingness and intention to awaken further is making the best use of your life, this wondrous opportunity you've been given.

We are part of a vast community of souls at our own states of evolution. Right now, you have attained the human form, the gateway to higher consciousness, to God. Don't let yourself be duped by your reliably wayward lower mind and its insistent desires. Rather, seize the moment. Be aware of being aware and turn within to God with love and longing. For that longing is stoking the fire that will burn away the dross—the veils that bind you and blind you from the living bliss and love that is yours.

Be in equilibrium. Hone your intuition. Grasp inspiration when it comes. Master wisdom daily—you can do it. Write in your Journey Journal. Be on purpose. Know love. Express your humanity. Connect with and enjoy kindred spirits. Cultivate commonality. If you are moved to, share your insights and appreciation on Amazon, Goodreads, and Facebook. Express yourself in your honest innocence with kindness. In this way, you encourage those you know and those you may never meet to further their own journeys and empower their nobler selves.

Make best use of this life, for this is rendering a God-pleasing service.

About the Author

Michael Goddart, MFA, is the author of *In Search of Lost Lives: Desire, Sanskaras, and the Evolution of a Mind&Soul*, a winner of the American Book Fest Best Book Award, the Living Now Book Award, the Body Mind Spirit Book Award, and the National Indie Excellence Award.

Soon after his family moved from Illinois to California when he was 10 years old, Michael started actively searching for the truth about death and how to attain everlasting bliss. He began daily meditation at age 19, and at 21 began to meditate for over two hours daily. His work as an international tax consultant and his spiritual quest have taken him to over fifty countries. Since 1974 he has journeyed thirteen times to India and also numerous times to England, Greece, Canada, Spain, and within the United States to be with those rare teachers whom he considers to be fully realized humans.

Michael Goddart took his MFA in Creative Writing at Bowling Green State University, Ohio. His other books include *BLISS: 33 Simple Ways to Awaken Further* and *Spiritual Revolution: A Seeker's Guide*, which the Hollywood Spiritual Film and Entertainment Festival named Best Spirituality/Self-Help Book.

Michael lives in Palm Springs, where he loves the warmth and the brilliance of the light, reading fine novels, and playing with his White Swiss Shepherd. Kindly visit www.goddart.com for interviews, excerpts, and endorsements.

CPSIA information can be obtained
at www.ICGtesting.com
Printed in the USA
LVHW030057241021
701337LV00004B/41